DISCARD

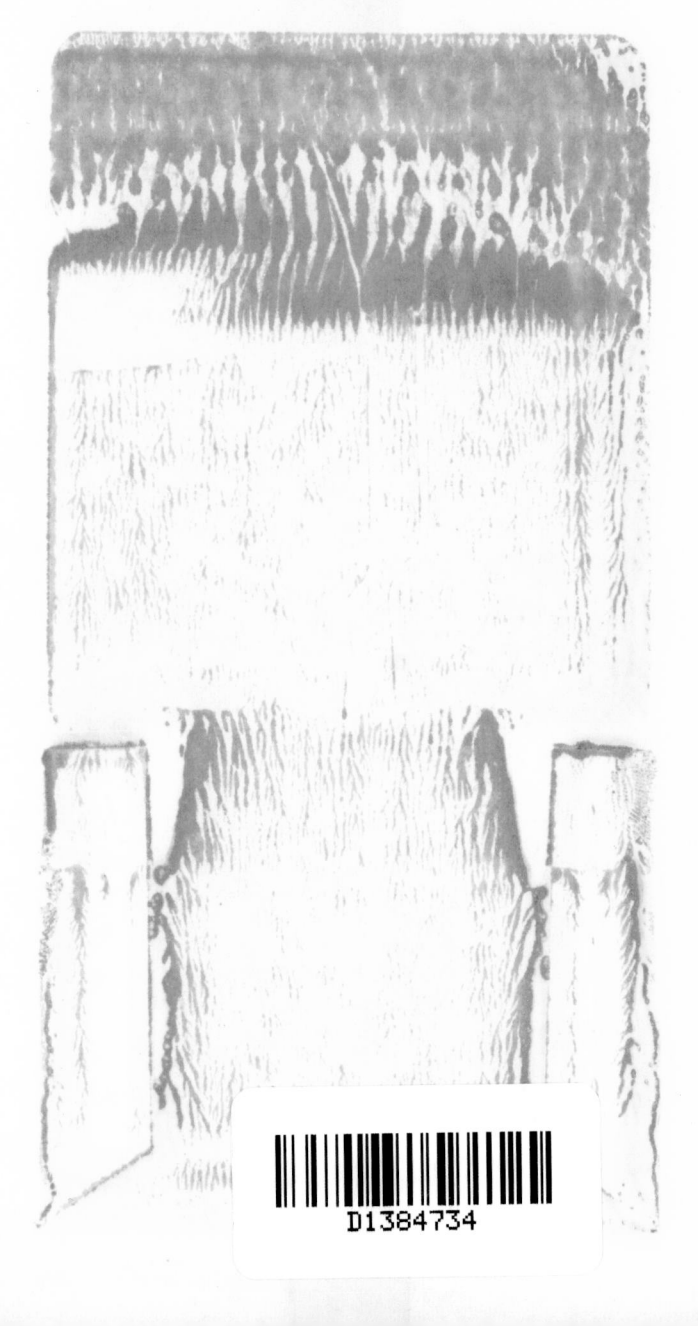

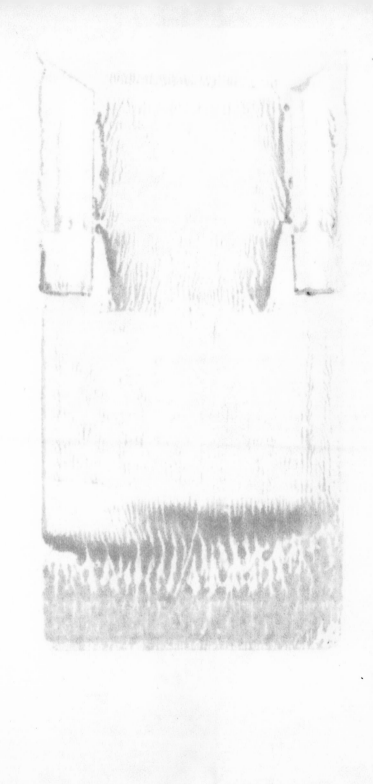

CATALOGUING
IN
PRACTICE

CATALOGUING IN PRACTICE

THE ORGANISATION OF BOOK ACQUISITION IN LIBRARIES

BY

FREDERICK BENNETT
ALA

LINNET BOOKS & CLIVE BINGLEY

FIRST PUBLISHED 1972 BY CLIVE BINGLEY LTD
THIS EDITION SIMULTANEOUSLY PUBLISHED IN THE USA
BY LINNET BOOKS, AN IMPRINT OF SHOE STRING PRESS INC,
995 SHERMAN AVENUE, HAMDEN, CONNECTICUT 06514
PRINTED IN GREAT BRITAIN
COPYRIGHT © FREDERICK BENNETT 1972
ALL RIGHTS RESERVED
0-208-01181-1

CONTENTS

LIST OF ILLUSTRATIONS

1

THE CONTINUING NEED FOR LOCAL
CATALOGUING

IN THESE DAYS of centralisation, automation and the large scale
library mergers brought about by local government reorganisa-
tion and business take-over operations, it is easy to ignore the
fact that much basic work in book-accessioning and cataloguing
must still be done locally in library workrooms. Many voices
have been raised recently in support of national cataloguing, on
the grounds that duplication of staff and effort is thus avoided
and consistency of practice can be maintained. This is very true
up to a point, and most autonomous library systems have now
established central accessions and cataloguing departments to
give their branch staffs more freedom to get on with their main
work of supplying books and information to the public.

The success of this local work-rationalisation has led to the
expectation that cataloguing can be taken over completely by a
national service, either at source before publication, or on legal
deposit through the national bibliographies. Moves have already been made in this direction by the MARC tape, the Library
of Congress and British National Bibliography printed unit
cards, standard book numbers, shared catalogue schemes and
library-suppliers' cards and processing services; but much re-
mains to be done before we can depend entirely on a comprehensive, prompt and adequate national cataloguing service.

Those libraries already using printed unit cards find they still
have to catalogue a large proportion of their new books themselves, since the national bibliographies are well short of a hundred per cent coverage; they have also found that the time spent

in altering the class numbers on printed cards to suit local needs, and in typing variant headings on individual cards (and in the case of card-charging libraries, typing or writing out each and every bookcard), is often more than that spent in typing complete entries for local duplication. This is a minor matter, however, compared to the far more serious holdup caused by the tardy appearance of citations in the national bibliographies and the MARC tape,[1] and the further delay in awaiting the arrival of the printed cards after they are ordered. This has left cataloguers with the continuing need for practical, cheap and speedy procedures for local cataloguing until dependable and prompt national services can be organised. These problems have been dealt with at length elsewhere.[2]

A further result of centralisation has been to deprive many young assistant librarians of the opportunity to learn accessioning and book-processing methods by experience; the larger the library system, the smaller the percentage of staff involved in accessions work, and the prevailing tendency to keep junior staff at service points without training-rotation through the administration departments confines accessions experience to the few permanent backroom workers.

Again, with the opportunity to opt out from the less ' glamorous ' subjects of cataloguing and classification in part 2 of the Library Association examinations, and in the fond hope that modern electronic and mechanical methods will save them from dull processing work, many accepted candidates for senior posts in local-cataloguing libraries find these hopes dashed and themselves inadequately trained to cope with the responsibilities of their new posts.

It seems to me that the splitting of library work into professional and non-professional categories has left accessioning in a limbo of unwanted duties. Chartered librarians consider the work to be beneath their status, and unqualified assistants feel that bibliography-checking, cataloguing and classification are beyond their powers. They are equally wrong; the work demands them both, and can give them more satisfaction than routine duties at the service points. After all, front-line troops must be supplied and supported by a dependable and efficient rear echelon, which can be justifiably proud of its part in the overall service.

There are some among us who have been deluded into regarding catalogues as white elephants of little working value, and which can be done away with. One argument—that the books themselves, if they are arranged in classified order on the shelves, need no listing—is a patently foolish one. Why do most library systems maintain interloans departments to deal with their hundreds of locally-unsatisfied readers' enquiries, and how could these departments function without local and regional catalogues? We can imagine the despair of a motorist needing a replacement valve-spring for his exclusive sports car being told by his spares dealer to 'search around the pigeon holes; there might be one there'. A printed, numbered catalogue would at least help him to order his spring with certainty.

It is true that a great deal of money is spent on the preparation and maintenance of catalogues. Some people hold that the cost at 5p to 8p per volume, is disproportionate to that of the books they describe, but the same argument can be used about the salaries paid to the staff who are employed in making the library's resources available, rather than to act as guards in a book-museum. Once the cost-effectiveness of local cataloguing is properly appreciated, routines can be devised to keep the costs as low as the locally-required efficiency-level permits.

Most cataloguers have formulated their own ideal work-plans, but the practical limitations of working accommodation, the shortages of staff and money, all force us to adapt to conditions as we find them and to do the best we can with the means at our disposal.

It is not my intention to add yet another manual of cataloguing and classification to the adequate existing textbook literature (which I assume has already been digested by the reader), but instead to supplement the theory, in particular, with working notes on rationalised methods which have been proven

1*

in the field by trial and error. This is a simple guide to what is actually done in some cataloguing departments, as distinct from what the textbooks say *ought* in ideal circumstances to be done. The field, in the main, is that of a large London borough system, recently compounded by the merging of three adjacent systems, each with different classifications and forms of catalogues.³ It is hoped that the practical methods outlined in the following pages will be of use to cataloguers and would-be cataloguers everywhere—not only to those in public libraries faced in the near future with regional mergers resulting from local government planning, but in expanding educational, industrial, institutional and special library complexes as well.

REFERENCES

1 Hall, A R, and others: ' Potential use of MARC records in three libraries ' (the Birmingham project), *Council of the BNB Ltd,* 1971.

2 Bennett, F : ' The independent cataloguer ', *Library Association record* 72(12) December 1970.

3 Bennett, F : ' Mergers and catalogues ', *Library Association record* 70(4) April 1968.

2

BOOK SELECTION AND ORDERING METHODS

THERE ARE SEVERAL sources of information which can be used as aids to choosing books:

For new publications:

1 the books themselves by way of pre-publication and approval copies;

2 the book trade periodicals (*Bookseller,* etc);

3 book jackets circulated by library suppliers;

4 publishers' catalogues;

5 literary periodicals, such as the *Times literary supplement,* Sunday supplements, daily paper literary columns, specialist magazines;

6 the weekly *British national bibliography* issues;

7 *British book news* and the National Book League lists.

For standard stock:

1 subject bibliographies;

2 the *British national bibliography* cumulated subject catalogues and its weekly issues for new editions;

3 the monograph bibliographies given at the end of *Encyclopaedia Britannica* articles;

4 reading lists prepared by specialist teachers, colleges and associations;

5 the bibliographies given in important or standard works.

The best way of assessing a book's worth is, obviously, to examine the book itself. Selecting new stock only from reviews, lists, book jackets or publishers' information cards is rather like arranging a wedding through a marriage broker, with the bride being kept out of the bridegroom's sight until after the register has been signed! Another argument for inspecting the book is the time factor; the approvals method has been found to be the speediest in getting new books into the hands of the readers, although some librarians pay scant attention to the speedy provision of new books—perhaps on the assumption that an uncomplaining public must be a satisfied one. This is a wrong attitude; a borrower has every right to expect to find a new book in his library as soon as a buyer in a bookshop. Using the approvals method and ' home ' cataloguing, it has become a normal routine in our system to release popular nonfiction, complete with full complements of cards, on to the public shelves within a week of publication date. Other systems following the BNB and review selection procedure have to hold up their orders for several weeks—sometimes for so long that some limited editions may even go out of print in the meantime, with little likelihood of a reprinting.

The approvals method requires the co-operation of one or more local booksellers in a reasonably large way of business. It is wisest to deal with separate booksellers for each of the categories: adult nonfiction, fiction and children's books. They should be asked to submit for approval each week either a comprehensive range of the new publications or a selection which they deem acceptable. Obviously, much depends on the briefing they are given by the librarian about his readership and his requirements, such as, for example, local bias in subject matter. A working partnership can be quickly built up and the most suitable new publications can be on display each week at the book selection meetings for the area and branch librarians, subject department heads and reference and children's librarians.

A very useful supplement to this approvals service is prepublication purchase. A good bookseller will permit—indeed encourage—a librarian to browse around his back store-rooms to inspect books not yet released for publication, and to purchase them on the understanding that they would not be put on the public shelves until their publication dates. These books can be married up to the approvals when they arrive in due course, and help to satisfy the requests for extra copies at the book selection meetings. This saves some clerical work in ordering and time waiting for the books to arrive from the booksellers. They can also be classified and catalogued in advance, so far as the manuscript draft, pending the addition of the branch locations to be decided on at the book selection meetings.

Before the approval copies are shelved for selection display they should be checked against the union catalogue in case some have been offered before, and also against the pre-publication shelves; it has been found to be insufficient to depend on memory alone, no matter how good one's bookmanship is. Each book is then given an order-card (Figure 1) headed by author and title, the right-hand margin bearing the location symbols of the branches and departments against which the selectors can put their ticks. At the end of each meeting orders are made out to the booksellers for all the extra copies needed; the approvals books, and pre-publication copies, if any, are passed on for full cataloguing treatment. If any of the titles displayed are not required, they are returned to the bookseller when his van brings the next week's selection.

It is obvious that the approvals method cannot be expected to satisfy all the needs of a library, but it does supply bookstock of a current and popular nature. Other books on the specialities must be selected by the staff, sometimes prompted by readers' enquiries, from the various reviews and bibliographies. The readers' adviser and the interloans assistant can often report a worthwhile book which has slipped through the selection net, and, rather than borrow it through regional co-operation schemes, it should be put on order if it is still in print and will fill a local gap.

Belated branch requests for books already in stock elsewhere in the system are ordered in the usual way, and the details added to the original order-card if that is still on file. The main entry in the union catalogue is copied on stencil for the

13

new branch cards required, and is marked with the additional location symbol(s); this also applies if extra copies to their existing ones are needed at a branch to satisfy a heavy local demand.

Author	CAPEL, Vivian		CB ✓	_AD_
Title	Public address handbook		BG ✓	_BR_
			MU	
			DO	
Publisher	Fountain Pr		SI	
Price	£3		WL ✓	_BR_
			SG	
Ordered from:—			WA	
Adams	25.x.71	Appr. copy	PO ✓	_BR_
Brown	26.x.71	3 copies	BO ✓	_JO_
Jones	"	2	FA	
Smith	"	1	RO	
			LI ✓	_JO_
			LA ✓	_SM_
			CU	

FIGURE 1 : *A completed order-card*

ORDERING

Each title to be ordered should be recorded on an individual order-card with the author as heading, or the title, if an author is lacking. The cards can be on differently-coloured stock to indicate the category; for example: blue for adult nonfiction and white for fiction, yellow for children's nonfiction and pink for juvenile fiction.

The function of an order-card is to act as the link between a book and its invoice—a transaction record of public or corporation expenditure to satisfy district or company auditors. It should cite the various booksellers involved, as well as the dates of the separate orders. After the titles on the cards have been copied on to the booksellers' order-sheets, the cards are filed by author in an ' on order ' tray until the books arrive. When they do, the booksellers' initials or code letters are added to the location ticks as completed, and nonfiction cards are transferred to

14

a section of ' current year's orders completed ' drawers, to be held against a possible auditor's check for the statutory period of three years. After this time they can be thrown away.

This means that five sections of drawers must be maintained:
1 on order
2 current year completed
3 last year completed
4 year before that
5 year before that (to be scrapped at the end of the current year).

This may seem to be a time-wasting chore, but once a completed card is filed it is merely a question of storage and of moving the files back *en bloc* once a year.

To save the typing time and stationery needed to maintain union fiction catalogues, the adult and children's fiction order-cards can be filed into a permanent headquarters union finding-list cabinet; we are thus able to get ' two for the price of one '. Branches can be left to catalogue their own fiction stocks as condensed author and short-title entries (see chapter 5 ' Name index condensation ', page 27). The fiction union order-card file must be cleared out by withdrawals notifications from the branches as in normal cataloguing practice.

The ' on order ' file should be examined each month for outstanding unsatisfied orders, and reports demanded from the booksellers for the reasons. If the books are out of print or otherwise unobtainable, the reasons are noted on the order-cards, which are then returned to the branches concerned and the booksellers' orders must be officially cancelled. Any catalogue cards which may have been prepared in advance should be scrapped after the relevant branch locations have been deleted from the main cards in the union catalogue.

COMPUTER ORDERING

The use of the computer in book-ordering seems at present to be more advantageous to finance departments than to the book-buying librarian and the bookseller; bill-payments may be ren-

15

dered easier, but more work is given to the library order-clerk, who still has to list all the books individually and to find their control numbers (standard book numbers or BNB numbers). There have been complaints of up to eight months' delay resulting from book-ordering by SBN and BNB numbers, and, in some education departments, of wrong titles being delivered, even though the control number was correctly given.

Author/title listings sent direct to booksellers are still far more satisfactory and there is less likelihood of receiving ' out of print ' reports some months later. Moreover, typographic errors are more likely to occur in typing SBN and BNB numbers than in copying author and title; meaningless chains of figures have less impact on a tired typist's mind than the immediately-apparent concepts of names and words. It is true that with this probability of error in mind, SBNs were provided with a built-in safety device, a ' fail-safe ' check-digit which supposedly triggers off the computer's rejection of wrong numbers; however, it is an unavoidable fact that it cannot replace them with the *right* numbers, and more time is wasted in checking all the way back to the original requests until the right numbers are found. As for the claim that less typing time is involved with number lists than with author/title lists, this has been found to be fallacious; on a test run, the extra care necessary with long-number typing and the scrupulous checking required afterward actually took up more man-minutes than the author/title list for the same books, even discounting the considerable time spent beforehand in seeking out the book numbers. It is to be hoped that future developments will ease these shortcomings, but we are not yet ready to abandon the more reliable author/title list.

3

CLASSIFICATION : GENERAL PRINCIPLES

UNTIL RECENTLY there were four or five major classification schemes in reasonably common use; Howard Phillips' primer[1] gives a concise analysis of each of them. Lately, however, most large libraries have used either the Dewey decimal system or its Brussels international modification, the Universal Decimal Classification. The British National Bibliography adopted Dewey as the basis for its classification in 1950 and is now using its 18th edition for both the printed bibliography and for the MARC tape.

Whatever classification scheme may be in use in his library, however, the cataloguer still has to conform to some basic precepts if he intends to classify the books himself:

1 To avoid personal bias and critical attitudes in classifying; for example, books about medical experiments on animals should not all be placed together in the ethics class unless they deal specifically with the cruelty to animals aspect. A medical student would give little thanks for such losses from his region of the shelves.

2 To keep shelf-numbers as short as the specific subjects permit and the size of the collection warrants, but foresight must be used in planning for possible wide expansion of the collection.

3 To place the books where they are most useful to the *borrowers at his library;* this is where nationally-standardised classifications such as those of the BNB and the Library of Congress often need to be adjusted to meet with local conditions.

17

4 To classify by the subject of the book in hand, and not give undue consideration to collections, series and learned societies as such.

5 To be governed by the *purpose* of the book; one about bees dealing with hive-making and honey-processing for the bee-farmer is better under agricultural industries than with entomology in the biology section.

A book's subject-content should not be decided by a quick glance and a snap judgement; title, chapter headings, preface and introduction, text and illustrations all need to be taken into account. Book-jacket descriptions are helpful, but can also be misleading on occasion. Before committing a book to a class number, the classified catalogue or subject heading in the dictionary catalogue should be checked to see how similar material has been dealt with previously.

If a subject is new to the library—that is, not yet represented in the subject index—the new heading is added to the index immediately and reported by a periodical subject-amendment instruction sheet to all branches, so that they may update their copies of the subject-index accordingly.

SPECIAL COLLECTION AND SUBJECT-DEPARTMENT CLASSIFICATION
The growing tendency towards the splitting-up of large general libraries into subject departments, and the consequent maintenance of subordinate departmental catalogues, should not be allowed to disrupt the general classification nor the union catalogue. Some keen specialist librarians may wish to rearrange the books on their shelves, and they should be permitted to amend their copies of the centrally-printed cards, but for the benefit of the wider readership over the whole system, the basic classification should be adhered to in the union catalogue. It is often best to restrain the more isolationist departmental librarians and to confine them to the classification in general use throughout the system.

Exceptions can be made when number-abridgement is possible. For example: a large medical department in a general library co-operating with a nearby teaching hospital could drop the initial 61 from its departmental notation; chiropody, normally labelled 617.585 would have this reduced to 7.585, and cardio-vascular anatomy would be shelf-numbered 1.1. This same number-shrinking could be applied to a law library by omitting the preliminary 34 from the notation. The few general books classified outside a department's specialty range but kept there for convenience would retain their full shelf-numbers to avoid confusion with the abridged numbers.

Some general libraries maintain special collections of books of local value but of very general subject-interest; these they keep apart from the main run of shelving. Many local archive librarians prefer to use their own specially devised classifications in place of the broader general notations, but records of their books should appear in the union catalogue classified according to the general scheme. Their presence is thus revealed among the books on the same subjects in the main collection, but the locations of the books are indicated by the added special shelfmarks on the union cards, or by a note: ' Located in the Special (or Local) Collection '.

PAMPHLETS AND EPHEMERAL MATERIAL
Holiday guides, time-tables, short-term material, reference pamphlets and so on need not be catalogued, but should be classified by the general book notation familiar to staff and readers, and kept in that order in file boxes or loose-leaf binders.

RECLASSIFICATION
A standard fixed classification requiring no updating has long been recognised as an impossibility; BNB did try to adhere to its 1950 classification, based on the pre-war 14th edition of Dewey, but had to abandon it after a twenty years struggle to maintain consistency. It is now realised by all that from time to time classification schemes must be amended and updated to include new topics, discard outdated concepts and improve existing subject arrangements in the light of new knowledge.

19

This periodic revision of catalogues called for by new editions of classification schemes and cataloguing codes can be carried out during the slacker publication months when the new books flow is eased. In many cases, reclassification can be dealt with by the proxy method (see ' Catalogue integration ', page 66)—that is, all those union catalogue cards which need new classifications or author-headings are re-stencilled with the modifications and card-sets are printed for each branch holding copies of the books. These card-sets should be sent out to the branches with this attached note :

' Please substitute these cards for your existing entries headed ....

and amend the notation on title-page and spine accordingly to : ....'

4

CATALOGUING : GENERAL PRINCIPLES

THERE ARE four questions to be considered by every cataloguer :
1 Is a catalogue necessary for his library in the first place?
2 What method and physical form should be chosen for his library?
3 Who should do the work?
For whom is the catalogue to be prepared?

' *Why* have a catalogue ' should be all too obvious; a librarian without one is like a navigator without a sextant, or a parson minus his Bible. A newly-enrolled reader given the freedom of a large library is a traveller in a strange country; he needs the signposts, maps and guidebooks of the classification scheme and the catalogue to help him find his way around the daunting array of many thousands of books. As I have already mentioned, some librarians have publicly doubted the usefulness of cataloguing, and argue that if a required book is not available at the time of asking, there is little point in listing it. This may be acceptable in a quick reference department, but it is far from adequate when readers prefer to wait for the return of the right book rather than be fobbed off with a substitute. The catalogue's function is to describe all books on the subject required so that readers have the opportunity to choose from them, and to reveal the right book for the reader despite its possible absence from the shelves at the time of asking. How many disgruntled borrowers have been lost to a library because they have only seen other readers' rejects on their subject shelves?

If they are not reassured by a percipient assistant and a demonstration at the catalogue that there are many better books which are on loan at the time, they may take away a poor picture of that library, which will probably endure. Let us criticise time-wasting methods of cataloguing by all means, but we should not kill the patient in order to eradicate the disease.

What method is chosen depends on the library service concerned; what is good for a municipal system with a large number of branches will probably be unsuitable for both a small technical library and a widely-scattered county library service. A factory library might prefer a dictionary catalogue to a classified one; a music library might need only a composer and author catalogue. The physical form: card, sheaf, printed, computer print-out or microform, must be chosen to suit the needs of the library's clientèle and the library floor-space available. A ten-cabinet row of card catalogues is accessible to several users at the same time; it is spread over a much wider area than is a microfilm reader which can be used by only one person at a time. So on first thought a busy suburban library may seem to need a card catalogue, but this might conflict with the need to conserve floor-space, and to provide maximum book-shelving and adequate reader-circulation gangways. The architectural consideration may therefore suggest that a microform catalogue would be sufficient for a popular lending library busy mainly with browsers. A long array of card cabinets might be better in the reference library thronged with students, if the cabinets were less expensive than a sufficiency of microfilm or microfiche readers.

Here we meet with another problem. Can we afford to maintain different forms of catalogues within the same system? Expense, speed and ease of maintenance, architectural requirements, quantity and competence of staff, must all be considered in catalogue-planning, as well as the simpler choice between classified and dictionary cataloguing. Even the varying *types* of catalogue forms must be brought under scrutiny before commitment. For example, if a microfilm catalogue is decided on, it should be borne in mind that as yet there is little standardisation of microfilm readers (although there has been much discussion of this lately[1]), and there is little hope that readers bought for the catalogue-display could be used for other purposes; other readers would have to be bought for those purposes. A decision would have to be made of film width from the three main stock sizes of 16mm, 35mm and 70mm; also a a choice between *cinemode,* which scans the film-roll vertically, and the *comicode* reader which passes the image horizontally across the screen; this latter has been found to cause much greater eye-strain than the former. It would be very satisfying to have a microfilm reader that could be used for local catalogue spools, regional union locations, periodical back-files, microfilmed standard monographs and so on. (Here is a worthwhile subject for the standardisation advocates to work on, both British Standards and the ISO: the all-purpose standard-film-stock microfilm reader, on the same lines as the standard compatible tape-recorder.)

Who does the work again depends on the service; in a small library it is very often the librarian-in-charge himself, but a multi-branch system demands a centralised cataloguing unit working alongside a stock editor, an interloans and regional co-operation section and the administration department. In such a unit, the staff should comprise a chief and an assistant cataloguer, two clerk-typists, an invoice-clerk and a general duties assistant as a minimum. All trainee-grade assistants should be seconded to a month's active participation in the work as a necessary part of their in-service training, so often neglected in many libraries. The staff should form a team as far as possible so that they can take over each other's tasks on occasion during holiday and sickness periods, and this should increase their work-satisfaction. There should be little room for the self-determined specialists who confine themselves to classification only, or to cataloguing only, and who consider typing stencils or counting books to be beneath their professional status. The work-flow in some systems has been seriously

23

inhibited by such displays of professional temperament—the ' who-tightens-which-nut ' syndrome so prevalent in industry today. A good librarian should be a jack-of-all-trades and a fountain of general knowledge; a good cataloguer is one who has worked as such a librarian at the public service points and therefore knows, by experience, what those service points need in the way of reader-guidance material.

A thought here on taking over already-established catalogues: some newly-appointed cataloguers who find their inherited systems not in accord with their own ideas attempt to reorganise them overnight. It is always better to accept their predecessors' methods and arrangements for a while and introduce changes gradually. The catalogue should never be regarded as a private training-ground on which to try out one's pet theories; it is maintained for the benefit of an accustomed staff and public who would be bewildered by sudden drastic changes.

It is important to bear in mind the readers for whom the catalogue is prepared. It would seem wasteful of effort and money to provide a descriptive catalogue complete with learned annotations for a small general library with a ' popular ' reader-ship, though some librarians have held that the smaller the col-lection the greater the need to exploit it by fully-descriptive entries. A large system, on the other hand, which includes in its reader-catchment area a university college, colleges of further education, teaching hospitals and the like, requires more than a brief author and title statement for its nonfiction, though the latter would suffice for its fiction.

REFERENCES

1 Williams, B J S: ' Miniaturised communications: a review of microforms '; Library Association 1970, p 56; *and* Burkett, J and Morgan, T S: ' Special materials in the library ', Library Association, 1963, p 149.

5

A PRACTICAL ROUTINE FOR CATALOGUING

1 AS SOON AS the books have been invoice-checked and process-stamped, new titles are examined by a senior cataloguer to determine subject-matter and classification number; this is written clearly in the process-stamp on the verso of the title-page.

2 The next step is the identification of the author's full name or the alphabetic heading for the entry; reference should be made to the catalogue for any previous entries under the heading to preserve conformity.

3 A manuscript card is written out according to a standardised layout, bearing all the required branch locations as indicated on the order card, and the necessary tracings for the added entries. This card is placed in its book and passed on to the copy-typist for stencil-cutting (see chapter 7 'A special cataloguer's duplicator' and plate 2). A suggested layout is shown in figure 3.

4 The cataloguer then checks the stencils against his manuscript cards for any typographic errors and marks the stencil backing-sheets with the quantities of each variety of print needed for each title. The make-up of a suitable rubber stamp for these printing instructions is shown in figure 4. The typist keeps the books in the same order as the stencils, so that when the cards are printed they can be inserted in their books without difficulty. The manuscript cards can serve a further purpose after the stencils are checked : to act as copy for the compilation of the next additions list (see chapter 13 ' The preparation of booklists ').

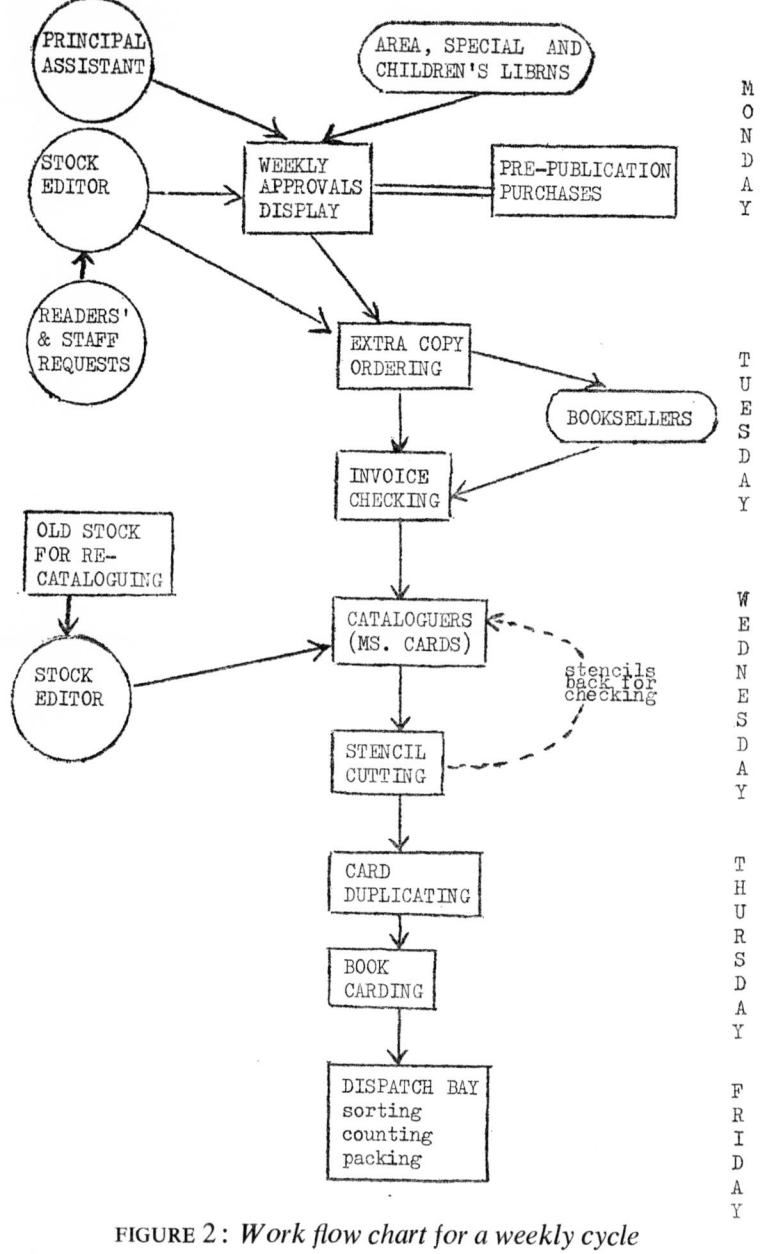

FIGURE 2 : *Work flow chart for a weekly cycle*

26

5 When the cards are printed, they are sorted into sets to be put behind the title-pages of the books in hand, and sets for the extra copies still on order and not yet arrived. The remaining cards, which are intended for the union catalogue itself, must be filed away before the books are dispatched to the branches; this will reveal any errors and queries in good time to retrieve the books before counting and packing.

6 The books, complete with their card sets, are sorted into branches and stored awaiting transport day when they are counted and packed. Delivery notes should be prepared on duplicate pro-formas: one to be signed and returned by the branch librarian as a receipt, and the other to be kept by him to furnish any annual statistic that may be required later for reports and Department of Education and Science returns. This receipt chit could take the form shown in figure 5.

ANALYTICAL ENTRIES

When these are required, as in the case of a book of collected plays or an anthology of biographies, contents cards are written out for stencilling, bearing the main heading (with continuation numbers on their top right corners when necessary) and a footnote is added to the main card indicating the presence of a contents list filed behind. When these contents cards are printed, extra ones are made for each specific entry for dissemination throughout the name index or dictionary catalogue under the individual headings, as shown in figures 6, 7, and 8.

NAME INDEX CONDENSATION

One criticism levelled at the card catalogue is that of its bulk; that every entry requires a 5in by 3in card to itself, and these, at the rate of one hundred to the inch of drawer space, occupy a large number of drawers which take up more valuable floor space. This defect, if it is considered to be a serious one, can be rectified in large part by:

1 maintaining only the one union catalogue at headquarters and confining the branch catalogues to their own holdings;

this also saves much unnecessary filing and withdrawal by branch staffs—it seems an absurdity to expect twenty branches to have to deal with perhaps the only book in the system;

2 condensing the name index whenever the slackening of work provides an opportunity. The collections of individual name cards of a prolific author and the biographical entries of a much-written-about personality can be reduced to cards bearing five or six one-line entries, as in figures 9 and 10.

This condensation can cut catalogue space by a third; it also speeds up reference to the catalogue by lessening the number of cards to be turned over. It has one fault in that it generates double sequences; the single-title cards stencilled after the condensation sessions have to be filed after the condensed cards. They are taken up in the next amalgamation, however, and this work has been found to be well worth the effort.

JUNIOR LIBRARY CATALOGUING PRACTICE

A children's catalogue should be made as simple as possible; young readers should not be daunted by the complexities of a classified catalogue with notation headings. At the same time, it should conform in essentials to the adult catalogue, so as to prepare the children for their later use of the adult department.

A good form of children's catalogue is in two parts: an alphabetic-subject section and an author section. A third subject sequence arranged by class number should be maintained at headquarters to aid the staff in stock review and book-selection.

It has been found that children's subject enquiries are invariably framed in basic language: farming is asked for, not agriculture; gardening, not horticulture. This is all very obvious, but some libraries still use the more pedantic headings. An alphabetic-subject catalogue built up with the simpler vocabulary has been found to be of more *direct* use to them, and encourages them to use the catalogues themselves instead of asking the assistant to help find their books.

The layout of children's entries can be simplified to render card-printing easier than for adult cards, as in figure 11.

641.5   CE   BG   WL

COX, Helen
    Mr and Mrs Charles Dickens entertain
at home; *with*: Dickens on food, selected
by S. McHugh

                    641.5

Pergamon, £2.50. 1970
214p; illus.

                 08   007108   2

DICKENS, Charles *and* Kate

823.092/DICKENS, Charles
(641.5)

O

FIGURE 3: *Main entry*

CLASS	
AUTHOR	
ADDED ENTRIES	
REGION UNION CAT.	
BOOK CARD	

FIGURE 4: *Stencil stamp for printing instructions*

.................Library   Date:

   RECEIVED for week ending...................

    Adult nonfiction ....   Donations ....

    Adult fiction —————   Revision items —————

     Total new books.........   Gross total —————

                          Pamphlets...............

         Discrepancies if any...............

             (for) Area Librarian...............

FIGURE 5: *Receipt chit*

```
808.82                    CE

MAYORGA, Margaret, editor
The best short plays of 1955-56
                              808.82
Boston, USA : Beacon Pr.   c.1956
305p; bibliogs.

FOR CONTENTS, SEE CARD BEHIND
```

FIGURE 6 : *Main card needing analyticals*

```
808.82  MAYORGA, M.—Best short plays 1955-56
contents:
         GURNEY, A      Three people
         MACLEISH, A    Music crept by me
         PERL, A        High school
         PERRINI, A     Once a thief
         PURKEY, R      Hangs over thy head
         ROSE, R        Dino
         SEIGER, M      Blue concerto
         WALSH, N       Let there be farce
         WILLIAMS, T    Something unspoken
         ZEIGER, H      Five days
ANALYTICALS
```

FIGURE 7 : *The contents card filed behind the main card*

```
WILLIAMS, Tennessee
808.82 MAYORGA, M.—Best short plays 1955-56
contents:
         GURNEY, A      Three people
         MACLEISH, A    Music crept by me
         PERL, A        High school
         PERRINI, A     Once a thief
         PURKEY, R      Hangs over thy head
         ROSE, R        Dino
         SEIGER, M      Blue concerto
         WALSH, N       Let there be farce
         WILLIAMS, T    Something unspoken
         ZEIGER, H      Five days
ANALYTICALS
```

FIGURE 8 : *Analytical version in the name index*

30

```
SHAW, George Bernard                    1.

    Back to Methuselah          822
    Doctor's dilemma            822
    Heartbreak House            822
    Music in London             788,25
```

FIGURE 9: *Condensed author card*

```
SHAW, George Bernard
    ERVINE, St J    Bernard Shaw            928/SHA
    McCARTHY, D     Shaw                822.092/SHA
    WEST, A         Good man among Fabians 928/SHA
    WINSTEN, S      Jesting apostle         928/SHA
```

FIGURE 10: *Condensed biography card*

```
FOOTBALL                        796.33

    CHARLTON, Bobby
        Forward for England
    Pelham, £1.50.  1967

FOOTBALL
```

FIGURE 11: *Children's full entry*

By merely masking out the subject-word heading 'Football', which is needed only for the alphabetic-subject catalogue (see plate 9), the stencil will then print all the other forms of card required: author, classified, stock-card and book-card. The subject-word is repeated at the bottom to remain as a withdrawal tracing after the heading is masked out.

31

6

CATALOGUE-CARD REPRODUCTION METHODS: A COMPARATIVE SURVEY

THE CURRENT computer-cataloguing trials being made in some large library systems do not suggest the likelihood of a general and immediate abandonment of accepted and established cataloguing methods. Even the universities have their misgivings about putting their records in machine-readable form, particularly retrospectively.[1] One librarian, Duchesne, poses a question very much to the point in asking ' In how many instances can we show really convincingly that library automation applications account for new service effectiveness or cost saving?'. It seems we must continue to maintain ready-to-hand card catalogues in our libraries for years to come. For a long time past the problem has been how to prepare cards quickly and cheaply. Both the librarian of the Library Association Members' Library and the editor of *Cataloguing & indexing* have declared that a large proportion of the enquiries addressed to them have been concerned with card-reproduction methods. BNB printed unit cards were intended to solve this problem, but, with delay in output and inadequacy of coverage, failed to achieve the success expected of them, so card printing methods must still be considered, even in BNB-subscribing libraries.

There have been few worthwhile discussions in the literature of card-printing techniques recently; those most worthy of consideration are by Pargeter,[2] Quigg[3] and Horner,[4] but although they are of interest to the student, their notes are of small value to the working cataloguer, who has to compare the

32

pros and cons of each method to choose the one most suited to his local needs. I have therefore brought myself up to date by carrying out a comparative work-study involving time and motion analysis, costing and end-product value estimation. This study was based on personal trials, manufacturers' demonstrations and frank reports from other cataloguers, municipal, special and university. In the following précis of this survey, cost per card refers only to stationery, materials and running costs at 1969 prices; it does not include staff time-rates, which are assumed to be fairly constant for whatever method of card-printing is used.

1 ROTARY WAX-STENCIL CLASS (Gestetner/Roneo etc)

Various layouts, from two to four titles to each foolscap stencil, have been used to print foolscap sheet-card which then has to be cut down to size and perforated for locking-rods. The printing is speedy enough, but there is an appreciable waste of time and materials in obtaining so few cards on a long-run duplicator. The initial outlay and installation of the necessary heavy equipment, such as a power guillotine and a jig-drilling machine, the concrete footings and extensive floor space they occupy, and the need for skilled machine operators, can hardly be justified unless they can be employed on home binding and other tasks. Another fault is that guillotine-cut cards are often wedged out into proud edges which make filing and finding difficult. Dagenham, and later Barking, libraries used the method successfully by laying out eight titles on a brief-sized stencil; for a system which maintains a union catalogue at each of its branches and therefore requires an unvarying number of cards per title, this is a very practical procedure. It must be remembered, however, that the end product is a unit card which needs to be given the required variant headings (class number, subject headings, added entries, by typing or writing them individually; the time spent on this and the subsequent checking of each offsets the speed of printing appreciably. Furthermore, for those libraries

33

2

still using Browne card-charging, bookcards cannot be printed from the stencils but must be prepared individually also.

Cost: 1p-2p per card.

2 ROTARY SPIRIT-TRANSFER CLASS (Banda / Ditto / Fordigraph etc)

These machines cost from £100 to £500 each to purchase and are reasonably simple to operate, but they are slower than class 1 machines. They do not give good legible impressions after more than 40 to 50 cards, despite the claims of some of their makers, as the characters spread and fade after approximately that number; spirit-transfer is not to to be recommended for books with a shelf-life of twenty years and more. These duplicators have the advantage over the rotary stencil type that they are able to produce variant headings (the Banda and Fordigraph in particular) by masking and ' variline ' techniques, but the users admit they are best for unit cards. As in the class 1 method, the smaller bookcards cannot register within the lay-out and they must be typed individually. I tried my best to put bookcards through a Banda, but found them printing slantwise and with amputated lines; time and material wastage was considerable and the machine was therefore passed on to the gramophone record library which required a less varied card output. Cost was higher than the Roneo class because pro-prietary material—special master sheets and solvent spirit—must be purchased from the makers.

Cost: around 2p per card.

3 EMBOSSED METAL AND PLASTIC PLATE CLASS (Addressograph/ Adrema)

Most libraries have now abandoned this method because of its poor legibility and registration, and its lack of sufficient setting-out space; the machines were primarily designed as envelope-addressing devices, and were not really convertible to the more demanding cataloguer's duplicator. They are speedy enough in printing, but initial delay—sometimes amounting to weeks—is caused by the plate-embossing bottleneck. The results are unit cards, although Adrema could take extra maskable headings on the plate; this, however, was a fiddling and time-consuming procedure. Initial equipment charges were between £300 and £700 but plate-embossing charges were extra, varying between £90 and £400 per annum according to the quantity embossed.

Cost: 2p-2½p per card.

4 SILK-STENCIL CARD-FRAMED CLASS (Addressal/Minigraph)
This method, as with class 3, gives best results in long runs of unit cards. Its limited aperture cannot afford a reasonably full entry, nor room for added entry tracings. As in the case of embossed plates, the stencils can be preserved for future reprinting, but very few cataloguers will appreciate this as an advantage. Equipment costs are £80 to £600; the rather expensive card-stencils are extra.

Cost: 2½p-3p per card.

5 OFFSET-LITHO CLASS (Multilith)
This is a sophisticated printing technique, requiring a £2,000 installation (for a 1250 model), an appreciably large working-area of twenty five yards by eighteen yards, concrete footings, power guillotines and drilling jigs and highly-trained operators. The great merits are speed and legibility, but this class also produces only unit cards, and is very uneconomic for a cataloguer's very short runs. Many local authorities have installed Multiliths in their municipal offices for council minutes, pro-forma stationery and so on, but I have yet to learn of library catalogue cards being handled by these printing departments as a regular contract.

Cost: 2p-2½ per card in 1970.

6 XEROGRAPHY CLASS (Rank-Xerox)
This does not demand a large installation charge because the equipment is rented at about £40 per month, with graded charges against the output through a meter. Because it is a

photo-electrostatic method, it gives facsimile reproductions, which naturally include any manuscript notes on the original; it is excellent for foreign scripts and type-founts. For normal cataloguing purposes, however, I found it impossibly slow, impracticable and expensive. As for the Multilith, the equipment and auxiliaries demand much floor space, heavy plant and concrete foundations; breakdowns, such as electrostat-cylinder stripping hold up production considerably while awaiting the firm's service mechanic, besides being expensive at £30 per cylinder. Highly-trained operators are needed, and legibility is sometimes below permanent catalogue standard, particularly when the cards have been insufficiently fused. As with most of the other methods investigated, it produces only unit cards, which require further manual treatment.

Cost: 2p-3p per card.

7 PHOTO-DYELINE CLASS (Azoflex)

Equipment costs are about £200, but there are extra running costs for the proprietary translucency masters, chemically-coated papers and developers. The standard coated paper supplied for continuous-strip printing needs to be cut up later to card size and punched for the locking rods. Legibility and performance are less than the spirit-transfer class, especially when the developing fluid is overworked as it so often is by the impatient.

Cost: about 2p per card.

8 MICROFILM PRINTING AND MICROFILM NEGATIVE SPOOLS

As a well-equipped practical photographer myself, I have been able to experiment with various methods of filming a grid of cards on 35mm and 16mm standard frame, covering a maximum of twelve titles per frame on high-acuity film. These negatives were legibly enlarged on bromide rolls, 5in wide (government surplus grade 4, contrasty), of continuous-strip paper fed under the enlarger from two parallel magazines. The results were brilliant and sharp, and, like Xerox, gave facsimile copies of the originals; but the whole technique is very slow and expensive. It requires specialised equipment and materials, highly-skilled operators and a darkroom. Pargeter[2] noted that the Evangelical Library tried to catalogue with a Kodak microfilmer (then costing £425), but had to abandon the attempt before completion as it had become impossibly expensive. Of course, for those libraries equipped with compatible microfilm readers, there would be no need to print the negatives down on to card stock; the negatives themselves, spliced into long lengths to form catalogue spools, are legible enough when fed, reversed, into the reader.

Such camera-produced microfilm catalogues could be of value in long-established institutional libraries and special libraries with static collections of incunabula and rare books; positive copies can be easily printed for postal transmission, and sales of these might help toward costs. For general libraries where bookstock is continually changing, the cost of insertion and deletion to update such a catalogue, either on card or on film, would be prohibitive. Another point to bear in mind is that a microfilm catalogue cannot avoid being well behind in currency because of production delays; even a computer-output microfilm lags two to three months behind accession dates. If a continuous-flow camera is used for card-copying, the cards can be overlapped to save wasteful blank space on the film.

Cost per card or per foot of film could not be calculated for my experiments; there were too many variables involved.

(*A microfilm production note:* When laying out the cards or copy for the camera, consideration must be given to the format of the microfilm-reader to be used; the text should read across the film for *cinemode* (the better framing) or along the film for *comicode*.)

9 AUTOMATIC TYPEWRITERS (Flexowriter)
Initial equipment costs are more than £2,000, plus a further £1,000 for a coding attachment. The Flexowriter is a typewriter giving off a by-product of perforated paper tape which can be

subsequently ' played back ' to retype the recorded characters at high speed any number of times as required. It can also be programmed for automatic rolling-back and spacing to provide added entries from tracings at the bottom lines of entries. This method, though too slow for quantity production, is excellent for libraries with limited requirements, and is giving every satisfaction in some university libraries. Its main advantage lies in its provision of paper-tape input for computer storage.

REFERENCES

1 Roberts, N: ' University libraries ', *Library Association record* 73(11), November 1971, p 210.
2 Pargeter, P S: ' The reproduction of catalogue cards ', Library Association pamphlet no 20, 1960.
3 Quigg, P: *Theory of cataloguing,* Bingley, second edition 1968.
4 Horner, J: *Cataloguing,* Association of Assistant Librarians, 1970.

7

A SPECIAL CATALOGUER'S DUPLICATOR: THE FLATBED SILKSCREEN FRAME

IT WILL BE SEEN that none of the methods described in the previous chapter can satisfy the average cataloguer completely. After all, the various machines described there were mostly designed by commercial firms for big markets, and to have a general appeal as long-run duplicators for business requirements. Some attempts have been made to convert them to library cataloguing use, but no specific ' cataloguer's duplicator ' has yet been offered on the market. When I submitted a design for a cheap semi-automatic cataloguer's machine to a duplicator manufacturer, I was told there are so few cataloguers it would be uneconomic to tool up a factory for only a few hundred duplicators. This I can well appreciate, and to satisfy the frequently-expressed need of our uneconomic few I have designed an even cheaper and simpler one, shorn of all refinements, and reduced to a basic construction that any handyman can make on his kitchen table in an hour or so, for less than £1. It has the following merits:

1 For six years, without breakdown or holdup, it has answered all my demands on it by providing all variant cards, including bookcards, for a large municipal system of fifteen branches, plus reference libraries and special collections catalogues, with an annual production of nearly 300,000 cards at $\frac{1}{2}$p per card.

2 It requires only a square yard of desk or table space, no electrical power point and is readily portable.

3 The technique of usage can be learned by any school-leaver or junior clerk of average intelligence in an hour or two.

4 Legibility and permanence of characters can be maintained up to two thousand impressions (not that we cataloguers ever need these quantities!).

5 Materials are non-proprietary and are readily available at competitive prices; there are no holdups caused by the non-supply of exclusive material.

6 Only the indicated number of cards need be printed, thus providing a check against books ordered, and avoiding waste of card stock.

7 All variant headings are given on the master stencil as tracings, except for a very few analytical entries; therefore the main cards convey all information, and nothing need be added by hand to any card except local book numbers and the occasional analytical heading. As all records of a title are identical, once the stencil has been checked there is no need for further proof-reading or checking for typographic errors—a really valuable saving of professional time.

8 Bookcards of any reasonable size are printed from the same stencil without difficulty, as well as non-SBN notification slips for regional union catalogues.

9 The simultaneous printing of six to ten cards per stroke (depending on fullness of entry) gives such speed that weekly intakes of five hundred adult and three hundred children's non-fiction book titles have been equipped with full sets of cards: classified, subject, author, stock-cards and bookcards, within two days of arrival from the booksellers.

CONSTRUCTION

The device is made from a 16in square multi-ply baseboard, which must be free from any warp or surface irregularity; to this board is hinged a hardwood frame 1in by ½in section, 15in by 7in external and 13in by 5in internal measurement. A taut screen of bolting-silk or screen nylon (eg no 8 seriprint) is glued to the under-surface of this frame (it is advisable to use marine

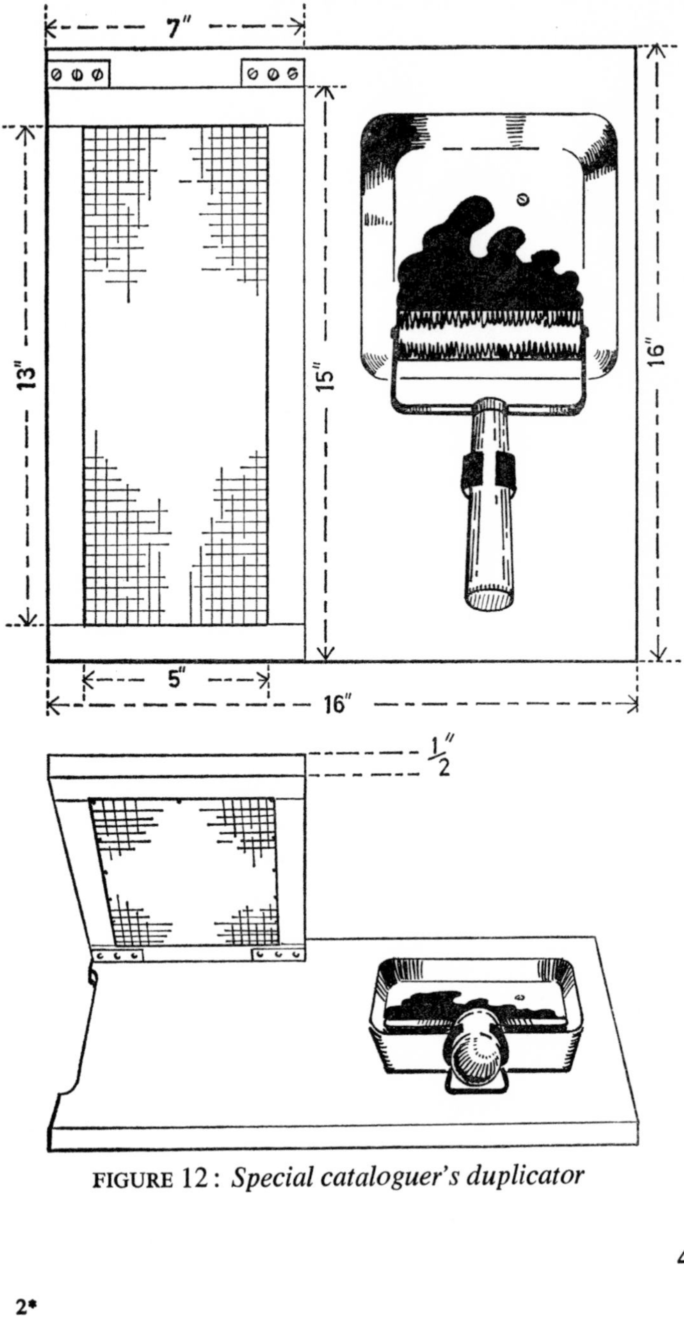

FIGURE 12: *Special cataloguer's duplicator*

2*

glue for this). When this is really dry, a 1½in border of metallised tape should be stuck on the underside of the frame from its outside edge to ½in inside the open silk screen. The frame may be hinged to the left half of the baseboard for right-handed operators or the right half for left-handed working. The inside long edge of the screen should be aligned with the incut edge of the baseboard and the outside edge of the frame with the projecting corners. The ink tray is screwed down with countersunk heads to avoid damaging the ink roller, and a clip should be provided to hold the roller handle captive when not in use, leaving the inky rubber roller in the tray out of harm's way. All woodwork should be given a coat or two of light-coloured enamel paint or polyurethane varnish to make cleaning easy and to reveal any unwanted ink-smears on handling surfaces, particularly at the bottom of the frame where it is held down during printing.

Screen-silk and ink-rollers may be obtained from any good artists' sundriesman. Standard rotary duplicator inks such as Gestetner, Roneo and Ellams are all suitable; rotary-cut (not guillotined), and perforated plain card stock, only slightly calendered, is advisable; if too highly glazed, the ink will smear more readily and if too porous the print will lose its crispness.

METHOD

Cut a standard foolscap stencil vertically down the middle and type the full entries down the strip (see plate 2) leaving 1cm between each entry. After checking for typographic errors and correcting where necessary, mark the carbon-copied backing-sheets with the number of the cards required for each variant heading (figure 4).

Remove the backing-sheet from the strip and hang it in front of the printer for easy reference to the card-quantity instructions; fasten a 12in by 6in strip of blotting paper to the bed under the frame by small tags of sellotape; this will absorb the first heavy inking of the silk. Place the stencil strip in position under the frame, making sure it overlaps the inside frame edges adequately to avoid ink borders. Hold the frame down firmly and roll the well-inked roller up and down the screen until it is completely black. Lift the frame and fasten a 12in by 6in strip of blank duplicating paper over the blotting strip; print down on this and mark it boldly with the registration positions for the various headings required; these marks should extend to the left edge so that they are clearly visible when the blank cards are laid down for printing.

When laying these down, begin at the top and overlap them, like reversed tiling. Print the indicated number of main entries first; if more cards are needed for isolated titles, mask off the neighbouring entries with scrap paper, but this can be avoided if the stencils are so organised at their cutting that titles with similar card requirements are grouped together.

On the underside of the stencil, mask off the headings no longer required with gummed paper strips. Lay fresh cards down at the lower registration marks to bring the author lines up to the heading position of each card; print off the author- and stock-cards, also the regional notification slips where needed.

Titles with added entries as indicated by the tracings are best left to the bottoms of the stencil strips to save the masking-off necessary when they are followed by other titles. Place blank cards with their top edges covering the required tracings on the marked guide-strip; overlap the cards if there is more than one tracing on an individual entry and print them together; shift the newly-headed blanks up to the top registration marks to print in the bodies of the entries underneath. Mask off each tracing when completed.

Lay blank bookcards down over the body of each entry and print them off.

If there may be a need later on to print extra cards, stencils can be placed ink side to the reverse side of their backing-sheets for preservation and easy identification; if care is taken, the masking strips can be peeled away to restore the main entry with all headings.

In children's cataloguing, if the simple layout illustrated in 'Children's cataloguing practice' (p. 31) is adopted, cards do not need to be repositioned on the bed to provide variant headings; the one easy step of masking out the subject-heading on the top left corner converts the stencil to author-heading, class-number heading, stock-card and bookcard format and only the one registration mark is needed on the guide strip for each title.

WORKING NOTES

In cold temperatures the duplicating ink runs thicker than usual, and extra pressure will be needed to penetrate the wax cuts; in very warm weather, on the other hand, the ink may flow too readily and seep under the edges of the cuts and spread; less pressure, less ink and blotting off the under surface of the stencil will remedy this.

If regional notification slips and small bookcards stick to the stencil when the frame is raised (this sometimes happens because they are much lighter than catalogue cards), they may be flicked off with the point of a knife; they should not be slid off, because this smears the impression.

The frame should always be lowered by hand and never be pushed down by the roller on the silk screen: this stretches the silk away from the frame.

As cards are printed, they should be laid alongside the frame in the same positions as on the stencil to keep each title's cards grouped together and in the same order as the batch of books flowing through the department; this saves much time when the cards sets have to be inserted into the books later on.

Cards should always be handled by their edges until they are dry; this usually takes two to three minutes. Criticism has been made that this method is a messy one, yet the same may be said about, for example, the techniques of painting and surgery —Turner and Barnard seem to have got by. An old Buckinghamshire saying is relevant here: 'Mucky does as mucky is'; if a clean discipline is followed and fingers and handling sur-

44

faces are kept free from ink, results should be brilliant. Paper tissues and ordinary soap and water are quite sufficient if fingers do become a little inky and the more genteel junior can always wear thin rubber gloves!

8

WITHDRAWALS, REPLACEMENTS AND STANDING ORDERS

SOME CATALOGUERS tend to forget that what is put into a catalogue must eventually be taken out of it, very often years later and when that particular cataloguer has moved on. Therefore, if added entries are made out, the relevant tracings must not be overlooked on the main card; otherwise the withdrawer of the future will not be guided to extract the added entries, which may remain as meaningless padding in the catalogue thereafter.

It was my sorry experience, on taking over a catalogue, to find that thousands of titles had not been notified as withdrawals during the war and post-war years. This was partly because a clear withdrawals procedure had not been drawn up in a manual for the staff—particularly the thinly-spread temporary juniors of that difficult period—to carry out. ' Sitting-in with Nelly ' has its limitations; instruction by official manual is far better. Errors in withdrawals can be cleared only by systematic stock-checks and calling books in for recataloguing, and it can take several years to weed out these ignored entries and so render the catalogue reliable once more. It therefore pays in the long run to be as punctilious in dealing with withdrawals as in filing new entries.

The main card, or the book card if there is one, should be used as the primary withdrawal agent (stock cards need to be retained by the branches for the obligatory three years district audit period). The classified catalogue is the first to be cleared; the branch symbol is deleted from the union main entry if there are other locations. If the withdrawn copy was the last one left, the main card is removed and laid aside for later deletion from the name index as the last copy in the system, and then sent on to the regional union catalogue stamped 'Withdrawn from .... Libraries '. If the card bears a standard book number, that alone need be sent to the region as a notification. The added entries of last copies must not be forgotten in both classified catalogue and name index, as they often are.

Fiction withdrawal can be a simple operation if branches are instructed to notify their last copies only; all that is needed is to strike the branch location off the order card in the union order-card file.

Replacements can be dealt with in the following elementary manner:

1 The branch librarian submits an order-card bearing the known details of author, title, publisher and date (this last can be changed to 'latest edition wanted '). The letters RPLMT (or other abbreviation) and the book number are written on the branch location line, and the request date at the bottom.

2 The original bookcard is also marked RPLMT and similarly dated, and is filed in a ' replacements ' section of the issue trays at the branch to facilitate the checking for reserves. These bookcards should be checked periodically against their dates for outstanding unsatisfied orders. The catalogues should be left unaltered at this stage.

3 When the replacement copy is supplied by the bookseller, the cataloguing department needs only to mark the title-page with the classification number and the branch's book number, and send it to the branch. Here the bookcard is retrieved from the issue-trays and the new purchase details are added to the original stock-card.

4 If the newly-supplied book differs materially from the edition originally catalogued, this new version is given full cataloguing treatment as a new book, and the branch is instructed to withdraw the original bookcard from the issue-trays and all the original entries from the catalogue. The cataloguing department clears its own union catalogue without waiting for notification later from the branch.

5 If the required book has gone out of print, the order-card is returned to the branch with the statement ' unobtainable ' and instructions to treat the book as a normal withdrawal.

347.058   WLref

    The LAW list

                    347.058

    Stevens
    Current copy

---

    805   CE

    The HUDSON REVIEW, *quarterly*

                    805

    N.Y : Hudson Review
    vol. X (1957) to date

FIGURE 13 : *Standing order main entries*

Standing orders, such as books supplied as serials or annual revisions, or bought on a subscription basis, need full cataloguing treatment only when they first reach the system; cards are prepared to cover these and subsequent issues. The accession details of these further issues should be noted at the branches on the original stock-cards year by year, or as and when they are published; the cataloguing department notes the regular arrival of issues by dates on the main cards. Two types of standing order main entry are shown in figure 13.

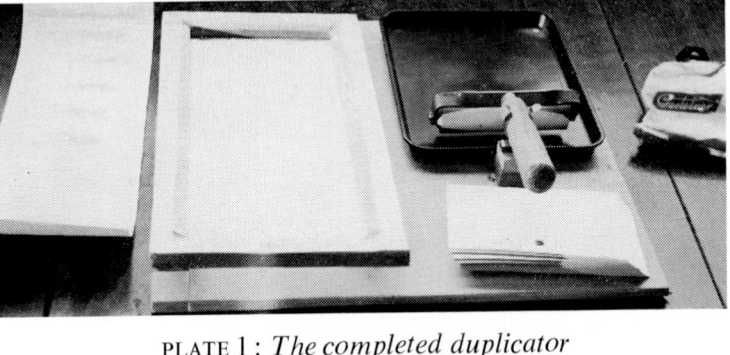

PLATE 1 : *The completed duplicator*

PLATE 2 : *A stencil strip*

[*facing p* 48

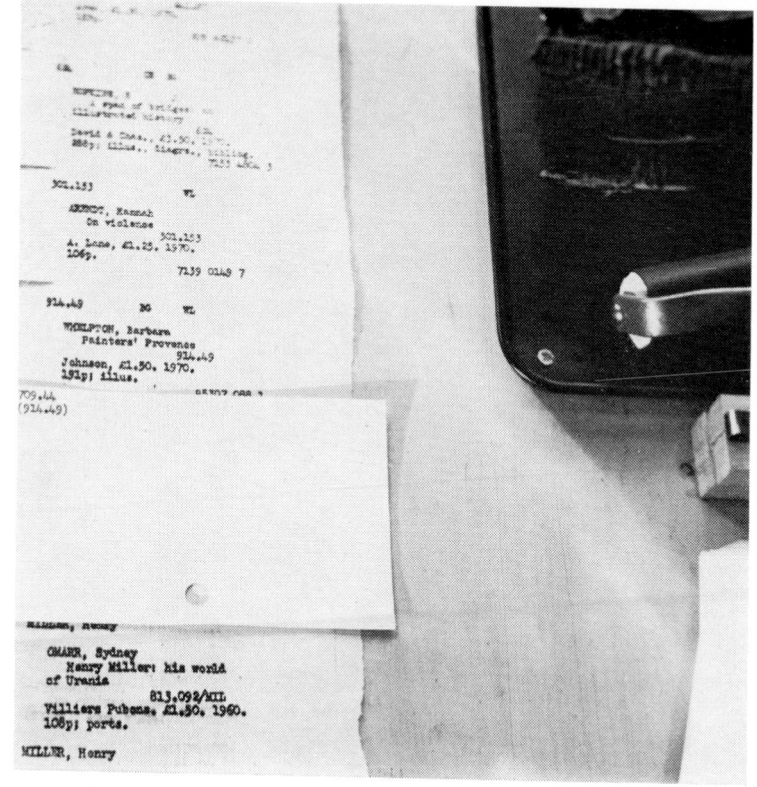

PLATE 3 : *Printing an added entry heading (classified) from the tracing*

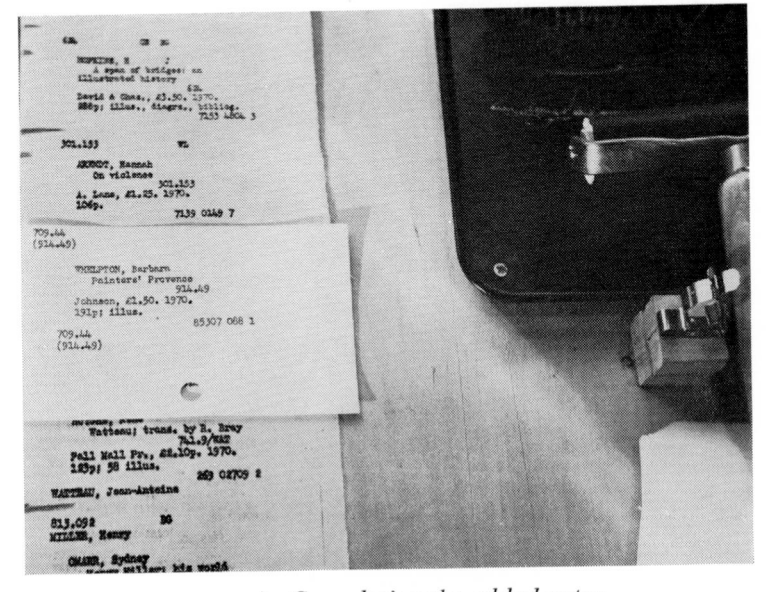

PLATE 4 : *Completing the added entry*

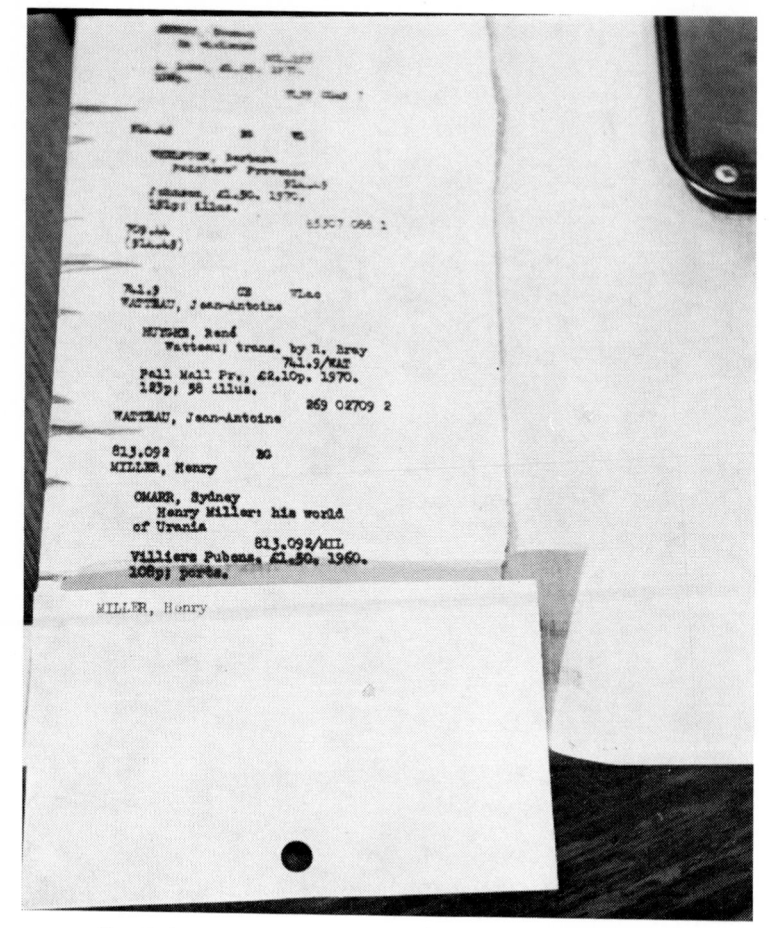

PLATE 5 : *Printing an added entry heading (name entry) from the tracing*

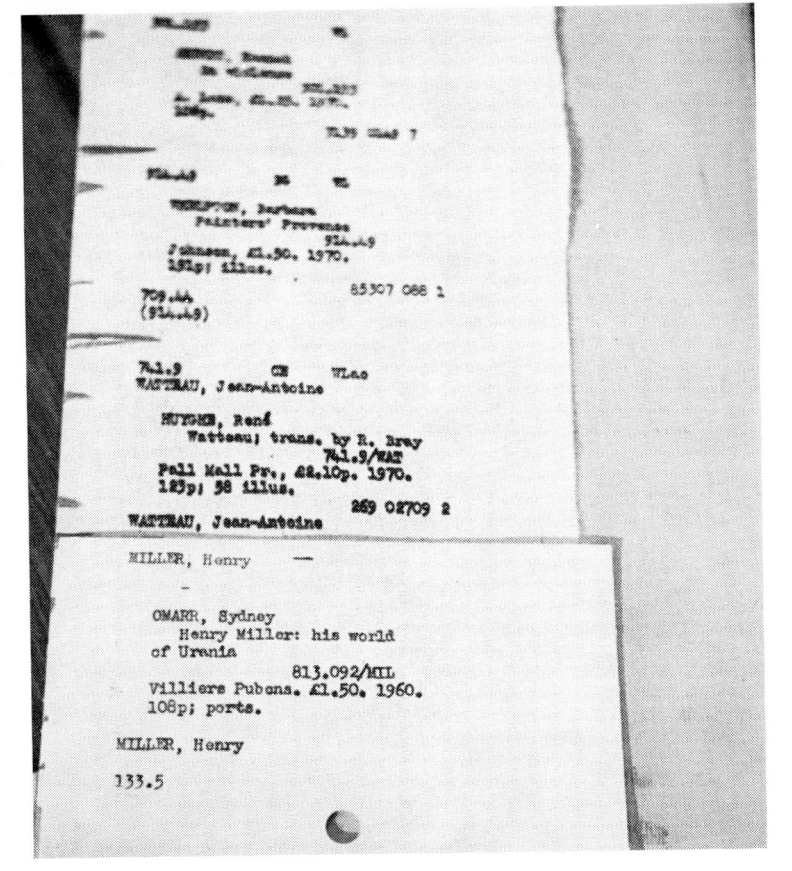

MILLER, Henry   —

OMARR, Sydney
    Henry Miller: his world
of Urania
                813.092/MIL
    Villiers Pubans. £1.50. 1960.
    108p; ports.

MILLER, Henry

133.5

PLATE 6 : *Completing the name entry*

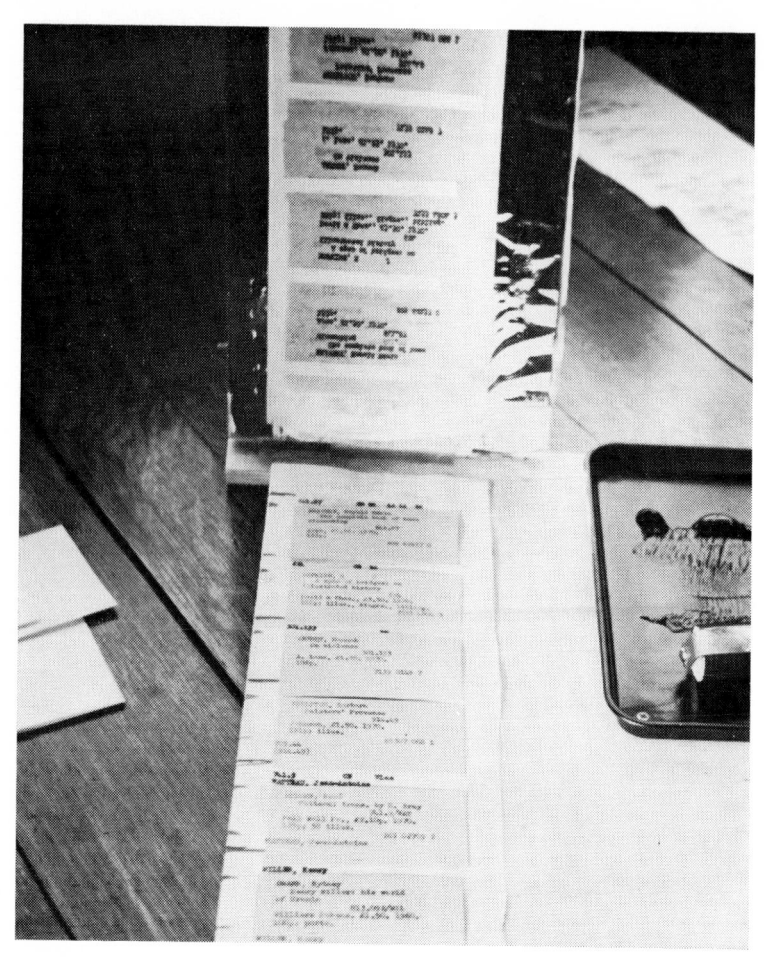

PLATE 7 : *Printing bookcards*

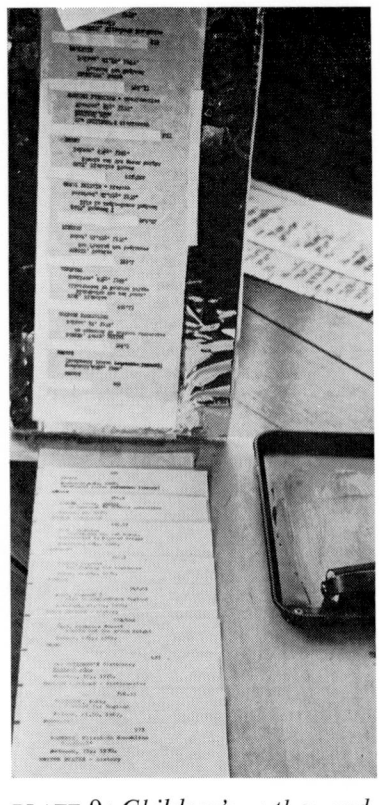

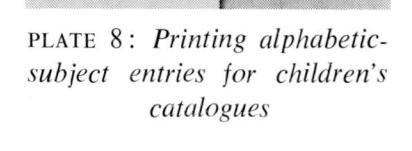

PLATE 8 : *Printing alphabetic-subject entries for children's catalogues*

PLATE 9 : *Children's author and Dewey cards after masking out the alphabetic-subject headings*

PLATE 10: *Printing children's bookcards*

9

ACCOMMODATION PLANNING, ORGANISATION AND FURNITURE

CATALOGUERS HAVE RECEIVED scant consideration from library planners and architects in the past; consequently we have to run our departments in any odd room or working-space not taken up by public areas, storage-rooms or administrative offices. A catalogue department's functional nature leads to it being considered as a domestic servant and therefore relegated, like Cinderella, to the servants' quarters in attic or basement. No cataloguer would wish to try to work in the bustle and limelight of the public areas, but neither does he enjoy exile to the inadequate backrooms and odd corners of some of our Victorian buildings. A little more thought has been given to this recently in planning for custom-built new libraries, but, as I have remarked in another context, most of us have to put up with existing conditions and to make the best of them by conversion and adaptation.

Sometimes an opportunity presents itself to transfer the department elsewhere within the building. For example, many municipal libraries of the Carnegie and Passmore Edwards category were designed with spacious newsrooms—a necessity in those sad days of widespread poverty and unemployment, when ' situations-vacant ' received more attention than Richard Dehan. Nowadays, television, radio and a better standard of living have lessened the need for large accommodation areas filled with newspaper stands and long tables flanked by rows of chairs. These newsrooms can and should be taken over by the less-well-housed departments such as cataloguing if they

49

can meet with the basic requirements: good location, accessibility, lighting, ventilation and structural suitability.

1 LOCATION AND ACCESSIBILITY

As the department handles the intake and dispatch of all the new books in the system, it should most conveniently be located on the ground floor, and at an outside wall of the building, for preference, to provide a loading bay big enough to handle large parcels and crates of books, and opening on to a side street free from traffic restrictions and loading problems. If this cannot be managed, the department should be located adjoining a lift-well so that book-transport in bulk can be handled without interfering with the running of the public service points. The department should also have easy access to all other parts of the building to permit full liaison and staff usage of the union catalogue, but it should not be available as a through right-of-way; the constant passage of other staff should not be allowed to distract the cataloguing staff.

2 LIGHTING, VENTILATION AND HEATING

Lighting is a matter of major importance in handling invoices, books and catalogue cards throughout the working day. Large windows, preferably of great width but shallow depth, placed high in the walls to accommodate shelving beneath, are the most suitable. Artificial lighting of the shadowless daylight type should be generously provided; there should be extra floor-points for desk-lamps, as well as for the ancillary equipment such as electric typewriters, electric styluses, microfilm readers and so on. There must be sufficient strip-lighting immediately over the catalogue cabinets so that users do not cast their own shadows over the open drawers.

Ventilation should be controlled by intake and exhaust fans of low noise volume. Heating has always been a problem in the usually crammed quarters given over to cataloguing departments; floor-standing wall-radiators take up valuable wall-shelving space, tend to buckle any books shelved near them, hinder the passage of staff and of book-trolleys; high-mounted wall-panel and ceiling heaters warm the heads of staff to the point of headaches and leave their feet to freeze; directional blower-heaters, no matter how quiet in operation, give a continuous soporific background hum which is almost an anesthetic in itself. It seems best to compromise; to have radiators as the main space-heaters and quiet portable blower-heaters as boosters in particularly cold weather. The radiators should be recessed into asbestos-lined wall-shelving and should not project into gangways where they impede book-trolley traffic.

Skylights are admirable for good uniform lighting, but can aggravate the heating problem; they can cause much discomfort in winter when they engender cold convection down-drafts on the heads of those working beneath; these drafts can be checked in a box skylight by a stout polythene screen stretched across its base, but a laylight should be double-glazed.

3 STRUCTURAL LAYOUT

There can be no ideal standard layout for a cataloguing department; everything depends on the shape of the floor-plan available. Basic requirements call for easy internal mobility with as few obstructing elements as possible, such as supporting pillars, fixed island furniture, machinery and equipment. The original layout will probably need altering later to adjust to changing methods and work-flow patterns, and book-trolleys must have clear gangways and turning-points; the department should be all on the same level to allow the easy passage of the trolleys and save the building of ramps at changes of level. There should be as few internal partitions and doors as possible; the doors should be of the hospital type (clear plastic flaps opening both inward and outward, spring-loaded) to permit the easy passage of trucks and book-trolleys.

Much has been said and written on the merits of open-plan architecture, and some modern libraries have made excellent use of such planning in their public areas. This has encouraged some librarians, prompted by their architectural advisers with

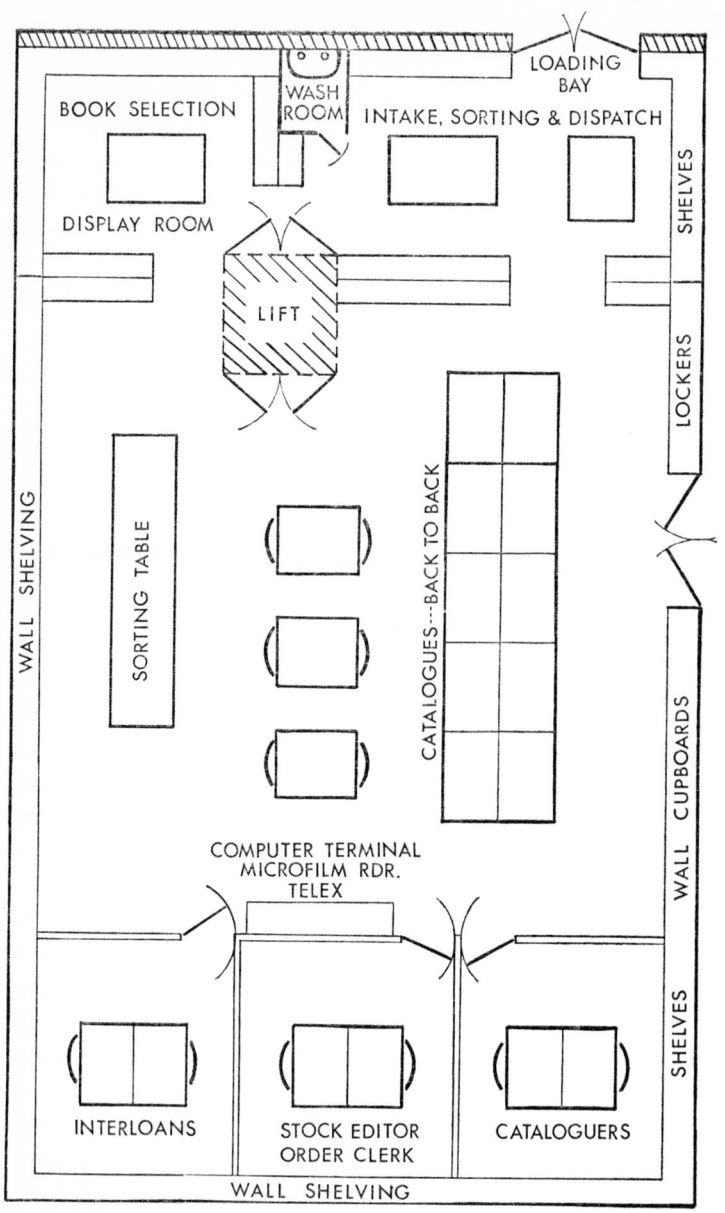

FIGURE 14 : *Basic layout for a cataloguing department*

apparently little knowledge of cataloguing problems, to believe that cataloguing departments should receive similar treatment in future library building projects. It has been said that cataloguers tend to develop a ' cloister ' complex shut up in their quiet little rooms (save the mark!), and would be much better off in the main hall surrounded by the rest of the staff. This is a nonsense; concentration on classification and cataloguing decisions needs a quiet room as much as a chief librarian needs undisturbed quiet for administrative decisions. It would be interesting to learn how many open-planners—architects and librarians—have liberated themselves from their own private offices, so closely guarded by ' engaged ' signals and private secretaries at the doors, and now station their own armchairs at ' the third rubber-plant on the left '. I can write from bitter experience of several years in open-plan, with crashing book-boxes, clattering typewriters, oral proof-reading and invoice-checking, and the working and telephone conversations of perhaps four or five sub-groups in the one hall of intermingled sections. Psychologists have admitted that open-plan working can lead to a progressive increase of noise and tetchiness on the feedback principle : voices have to be raised to be heard over the background level and other voices need to be raised accordingly; tempers rise with the voices, and work and staff-relations suffer. The open-plan advocates have recognised this noise-disturbance factor but claim it can be diminished by low acoustic-panelled ceilings and deeply-carpeted floors, thus alleviating one ill by inducing others. Low ceilings deprive us of some badly-needed wall-shelving, natural lighting and good convection ventilation; foam-reinforced thick-carpeted floors are poor running surfaces for heavily-laden book-trolleys.

The good cataloguer does not spend all his time at ease in his private study, but only that part of his working day on the tasks requiring concentration. An open-plan hall is suitable for the clerical and routine work, and of course a union catalogue in card form demands a large area to itself, but open-plan departments have been found to encourage an excess of social conversation, and for this reason a glass partition between the quiet room and the main hall is a psychological deterrent to overmuch time-wasting, as well as an aid to good lighting. If one is not already close at hand, a wash-closet should be built in a convenient corner; dirty parcels, dusty old-stock books for revision and card-reproduction work make this a necessity. A book-traffic plan should be worked out and drawn up to organise the circulation of books in a logical time-saving flow, and shelving and desk-arrangement distributed accordingly.

4 FURNITURE

Adequate shelving is the most important consideration; too many existing catalogue departments struggle on from year to year with an insufficiency of shelves, and books are left still packed in their delivery parcels on the floor until shelves can be cleared of the books receiving current treatment. This is not only a waste of floor space but it also creates obstacles to mobility around the department, and time and energy is spent in continually moving books backward and forward. Wall shelving does not intrude into the working areas as do island bookcases, but thought must be given to the wall area taken up by doors, windows, stationery cupboards, clothes-lockers and the like. Alcove shelving is not recommended, for it inhibits traffic-flow around the department.

Tables and desks: a long refectory table (ten to twelve feet) is most useful for sorting and putting into order large consignments of old-stock revision books and as a general work-table; smaller sturdy tables should be provided for the book-packing and processing areas. An ordinary flat-top office desk without book shelves should be available for each senior worker; the knee-holes must be large enough to accommodate the chairs when not in use to keep gangways clear. Rounded corners are recommended for all desks and tables to avoid bruising staff, trolleys and books on their passage round the department.

Chairs should not be the deeply-upholstered swing armchairs of the heavy executive type; these may be excellent for board meetings after a lavish lunch, but not for a busy cataloguing staff. Cataloguers spend surprisingly little time sitting down; we are constantly getting up to consult catalogues or bibliographies and visiting widely-spread shelves following the work-flow, so although chairs should be comfortable enough, they should be light and free from arm-rests, which can be more of a nuisance than an aid and comfort. A *filing stool* on wheels is a wise investment when long periods of filing have to be endured, but a flat-top trolley makes an excellent substitute which economises on both money and space.

Book trolleys: two types are needed : a flat-top, three feet long by two feet six high, to transport books lying on their fore-edges, and a display trolley, three feet six long by four feet high with inward-sloping shelves each side for desk-side work. The flat-top can be used as a mobile working table as well as for its designed purpose and as a filing seat; the display trolley conveys books in arranged order from the shelves to the desks of invoice-clerk and cataloguer.

Miscellaneous equipment: should be restricted to the necessities. In my junior days, I served under a very gadget-minded senior who was easy prey to the blandishments of a persuasive library-supplies salesman; years later, while clearing out much-needed cupboard space, I found many of these ' aids ' had hardly been used, if ever. We must be ruthless in rejecting any machine or gadget that is not paying its way in the department; it must not be allowed to occupy working space merely because it looks impressive.

10

ACQUISITION AND CATALOGUING IN SCHOOL LIBRARIES

VERY FEW SCHOOL LIBRARIANS and teachers are given the opportunity to select their new books from approval copies; the book-ordering routine adopted by most local education authorities is to select from suppliers' lists, publishers' catalogues, the *Bookseller* and the various reviews, notably those in the *Times educational supplement* and the *School librarian*. The official ordering is done by standard book numbers on triplicate forms designed for computer-ordering; non-SBN titles have to be ordered on separate forms—sometimes in quintuplicate. The recent trend towards the amalgamation of smaller education authorities into the much larger regional and county bodies has determined this centralised routine of book-purchase. Because of the large administrative areas involved, very few school librarians and teachers can be permitted to leave their understaffed schools to visit their local education authority headquarters for a weekly or even a monthly approvals book-selection meeting, particularly from schools in the country areas. Some library suppliers do send travelling collections around for inspection, but their circuits are so large that rarely can the books be entitled to the designation ' new '; in fact, some suppliers insert reprints in these collections. This calls for a great deal of catalogue-checking to avoid the unnecessary duplication of titles and the expenditure of limited capitation funds, at present averaging only 50p-£1 annually per scholar.

Ordering by SBN, as noted elsewhere, has proved unsatisfactory in some respects. Some school librarians of my acquaintance have told me of wrong titles supplied from their SBN order-sheets, of many ' no trace ' returns by the LEA computer (although a few of these were occasioned by misprints of SBNS in the *Bookseller* and the reviews), and of lengthy delays in supply—sometimes more than three months. School librarians have found the resulting checking-back to find the correct SBNS to be a very onerous task which prevents them getting on with their main work. As one educationalist has said : ' To oblige trained librarians to spend their time on non-professional work is uneconomic '.[1]

It would help school librarians and teachers if LEAs could be persuaded to decentralise a little and provide local approvals-selection centres within easy travelling distance of the schools; this could be a very practical proposition in towns and cities, where public librarians have found absence from their libraries for one afternoon a week to select their books to be very worthwhile.

A certain amount of the non-professional work in book-accessioning can be entrusted to the pupils; this has been done in the children's departments of many public libraries, to the benefit of both staff and children. The clerical work involved in the writing or typing of order-cards, book-labelling and jacketing is well within the capabilities of the upper forms. This work should be given only to trusted regularly-appointed library monitors; the school librarian should not be expected to depend on casual and conscripted labour. It is frustrating to lose good assistants as soon as they become productive after a sometimes lengthy period of training. In appointing library monitors at the beginning of the school year, it is worth remembering the old maxim : one volunteer is worth a dozen pressed men. Some of us may have experienced a lack of interest among the pupils, but this should not make us cynical; if the right approach is made, they will be more than forthcoming. I myself have found their enthusiasm almost an embarrassment in their clumsy but well-meant efforts (though I refrained from telling them so!). Hammersmith County School for Girls had a team of twenty five monitors who sorted catalogue cards and filed them, as well as discharged and issued books (annual issue 15,000); in addition to these monitors, teams of different girls enthusiastically unpacked and processed new books in their lunch times. So popular was this work, it seems, that there had to be special library-duty rotas.[2]

School libraries serve much the same purpose as public libraries: to provide general background reading. Textbooks provided for class-work are in the care of the heads of departments and the specialist teachers, and should have no place on the library shelves. Unlike the public library, the school library has to serve two very different kinds of user: the purposeful teacher who sets topic- and project-tasks for his pupils (and who also needs his own personal background reading), and the self-motivated pupil with hobby-interests. Both require the guidance of adequate classification and cataloguing, which few school libraries possess. Some have no catalogue at all and only a rudimentary colour-code classification in very broad groups of travel, science, history and so on. R J Hoare[3] writes: ' Even if the books are deployed throughout the school so that children are surrounded by them, they should still be classified and catalogued, which will allow someone . . . to learn of their existence in the school and locate them . . . I don't mean coloured strips of paper on their spines, but classified according to Marjorie Chambers's *Abridged Dewey Decimal classification,* which works *even with seven-year-olds'* (my italics).

This is sound commonsense, so long as a simple but thorough alphabetic-subject index is provided. A catalogue similar to that described on page 28, under ' Junior library cataloguing practice ', has been found to be better still: an alphabetic-subject section with an author sequence, plus a decimal classified catalogue for book-selection purposes and teachers' project work. Some school librarians have found a need for a title index more pressing than do public librarians who have the British national bibliography to hand; this in any case does not provide such a quick single-sequence search as does a library's index of its own limited stock. To economise in cabinets and card stock, this index could be written or typed on half-cards (3in by 2½in), as it need give only short entries: title, author, shelf-mark. In those libraries using the flat-bed card-printing method, it is an easy matter to produce a title-card variant by repeating the author after the title on the stencil and masking out the author heading after all other cards are printed (see page 44).

At present, the majority of school librarians maintain only the one simple catalogue and thus have no need to concern themselves with card-duplication, but the increasing build-up of the larger educational institutions, such as 2,000-place comprehensive schools and colleges of further education suggests that some thought is needed for the future. These larger schools might require departmental libraries on the lines of the subject departments in some public libraries; even if the books are all housed in the one school library, department heads should be supplied with copies of the subject cards of their specialties. Furthermore, most schools issue books for home reading, and some issue-records have been badly managed in the past in their tatty copy-book registers. The public library card-charging system is increasing in popularity, and if a flatbed duplicator is used, there is no problem in printing bookcards as well as all the other cards needed for each title: author, subject-word, class number, title, stock-card and departmental copies. Most schools have a handicraft workshop: here is an excellent opportunity for departmental co-operation and library-interest building by suggesting pupils should construct a flatbed duplicator themselves and use it for library purposes. One of my abiding joys, campanology (bell-ringing), was started off at school by my engineering teacher giving me the task of making-up and founding a bell-metal alloy; he then asked me to turn the ingot on a lathe to form a bell. Who knows what future Caxtons and William Morrises may be inspired by a card duplicator made with their own hands?

The school librarian is expected to produce booklists for all departmental heads: a monthly one of new accessions in general, and periodical subject-lists of relevant books in stock for each department; this latter is important in schools subject to frequent changes of staff, and should be updated as often as possible. If the lists are lengthy and enough copies are circulated to justify their duplication, this can be done on the commercial department's rotary duplicator after being made up as described below in chapter 13. Pupil co-operation in this can be very satisfying to all concerned; the English Department might cast a favourable eye on the work as a likely project; so would the Commercial Department. If the school possesses an Adana or other printing press in the Technical Department, the work could be contracted out there.

REFERENCES
1 Moor, E L: ' Staffing of secondary school libraries ', *School librarian,* March 1971, p 12.
2 D Warren: ' The library in a London comprehensive school ', *School librarian,* March 1970, p 2.
3 Hoare, R J: ' Finding the answers ', *Times educational supplement* 13th February 1970, p 46.

11

ACQUISITION AND CATALOGUING IN SPECIAL LIBRARIES

SPEED IN BOOK PREPARATION is even more important in special libraries than in general libraries. Manuscripts take nearly a year in passing through the publishing process, and by the time they achieve print the information they contain may well be out of date, particularly in the case of scientific and technological material, reports, research papers and pamphlets.

New-book selection should therefore not be delayed by slow routines, inhibited by list-circulation through departmental in- and out-trays. Naturally, the advice of all subject-specialists should be sought, and the lists should be considered by an active selection committee, but the final choice—and a quick one—should be the responsibility of the librarian; this will get orders placed with the minimum of delay.

Paradoxically enough, too much dependence on the best reviews can be fatal in procuring very specialised monographs. As these reviews may appear in print so long as a year after publication dates, the journal dates may give a wrong impression of the currency of the books reviewed. In fact, the books may have even gone out of print in the meantime owing to the limited print-orders often allotted to specialised literature.

Approvals-ordering, as described in chapter 2, is by far the best and quickest method; a co-operative bookseller with an eye to regular and assured trade will keep watch for any stipulated limited-subject literature appearing and about to appear. To supplement this source, use must be made of publishers' classified lists, book trade periodicals, the weekly BNB and the various guides to the literatures of special subjects, although these latter are rarely sufficiently up-to-date. Advantage should also be taken of the large quantity of free and trade literature offered by many industrial concerns; these items are not announced in the usual journals and can be easily overlooked if they are not directly offered to the library, or solicited under a special subject blanket-request by the librarian.

Ordering procedure is best organised by the order-card method outlined in chapter 2. In view of the lengthy delays in book-supply encountered in ordering special library material, particularly in foreign languages, it is necessary to check the 'on-order' file carefully before ordering in case the item has been ordered already months before and forgotten. Again, if acquisitions are heavy, the order-cards should be checked against the books in hand being processed.

Periodicals form a most important part of a special library's holdings; they contain much up-to-date information which is only infrequently reprinted in book form, and that usually too late to be of value. They should be obtained as 'standing orders' (see chapter 8), and a receipt-file record maintained on a visible records index such as Kardex, Wheeldex or Shifdex, to keep a vigilant eye on the regular receipt of issues, parts and continuations. If these business aids are considered to be unnecessary in a small library, a simple 5in by 3in receipt-record card can be filed immediately behind the main standing-order entry in the catalogue. When parts or issues are bound together in permanent book form, these bindings should be noted on the cards and they can thereafter be treated as books, but until this is done, the separate issues should be kept in file boxes to avoid damage and dust; if they are thin enough they can be clipped in spring-back binders.

Classification has always been an acute problem in special libraries. Some centuries-old institutional libraries have no subject classification at all, but shelve their books by accession numbers; subject-guidance is provided by alphabetic subject-card catalogues. The published schemes for general libraries, such as standard Dewey, UDC, Bliss and Library of Congress, can be adapted to special library usage by notation-pruning (see page 18), but many special libraries prefer to use schemes published for their own subject-ranges: SfB for building, Barnard for medicine and so on. Others have developed their own private classifications and see no need to abandon them to conform to outside pressures for standardisation. The heavy workload involved in revising large stocks to a new classification is rarely considered justifiable in an autonomous library, but thought should be given to the prospect of any mergers with other libraries, firms or institutions in the future. If these mergers eventuate, the integration procedure outlined on page 66 may be applicable.

The call for classification-standardisation as an aid to inter-library co-operation seems less relevant now with the advent of standard book numbers; the subject-fields of most special libraries are implicit in their names, and individual books are never requested by classification numbers. The future development of SBNs on the Continent, with Germany already active and France preparing to adopt them, may speed up book retrieval when the large foreign book intake needed by special libraries is eventually identity-numbered in BNB and MARC, *Biblio* and all the other major bibliographies.

Cataloguing in special libraries should be as full and complete as possible if the catalogue is in printed, sheaf or card form. If the library has computer-access however, and wishes to convert to computer-cataloguing, a COM (computer output microfilm) catalogue might necessitate short one- or two-line entries, although if 30,000 of these can be printed on a 3,000-frame spool or cassette, there is no reason why 15,000 entries twice as long should not be accommodated. We must bear in mind, however, that the pressing need for currency in a special library catalogue would be poorly served by months-long delays in updating, and that cumulation-runs on COM can be prohibitively expensive when the costs are not shared by a large number of subscribers.

A small bookstock requires a detailed catalogue to exploit it fully, with as many added entries, analyticals and references as might be deemed necessary. This comprehensive cataloguing is best managed in a card catalogue, although in those libraries where speedy updating of catalogues is not considered vital (for example, of subject-fields in which new titles are infrequently published), a printed catalogue is better both for its speed of scanning and its facility of widespread distribution among clients and affiliated bodies. This is where the printed catalogue scores; copies can be sent to all departments of the organisation no matter how decentralised they are; the client does not have to visit the library to consult a card, sheaf or microform catalogue for a known book or subject. The majority of the smaller special libraries appear to prefer the card catalogue as the main record however, and publish periodically updated special subject-lists for circulation to outlying departments.

Because of the predominance of local classification schemes and local modifications in special libraries, and the fact that much of their intake is not covered by BNB, printed cards are seldom used. The smaller libraries needing only four or five cards per title can manage by typing them, but if they are long entries (and special library cards often bear notes, contents-statements and abstracts), they are worth duplicating on a Minigraph or similar small duplicator to produce unit cards. If several variant headings are needed for each title, the flatbed method is best, particularly when branch and outlier catalogues have to be maintained. Some special libraries in large organisations are fortunate in having access to document-reproduction and printing equipment in other departments of the firm or institution, such as Xerox, offset-litho and other heavy and expensive plant which general libraries rarely employ; unit-card printing could be farmed out to these printing departments if costing and end-product value make it a worthwhile proposition.

Periodical indexing and abstracting are most important functions of the special library. In some libraries, more than 60 per cent of the book fund is taken up by the purchase of journals and magazines; to extract the utmost benefit from this current material, it should be thoroughly indexed for circulation to all departments inside the organisation and, outside it, to affiliated bodies. This work usually devolves on the cataloguer. Several national and international co-operative indexing projects are now being carried out; one of the best examples to my knowledge is the FIAF (Federation Internationale des Archives du Film) scheme, which has produced two comprehensive manuals on the standardisation of indexing and filing procedure for its subscribing libraries, besides a third volume of special film-subject headings in English and French for film libraries. These manuals are models of their kind, and could be copied to great advantage by other affiliations of special libraries. The scheme in brief commits each member-library to purchase a number of specified periodicals (much like the Metropolitan Special Collections scheme for books), and to the responsibility for providing indexes of these on standard forms for headquarters, which in return distributes complete sets of index cards to its members throughout the federation.

12

CATALOGUE INTEGRATION FOR AMALGAMATING LIBRARIES

WHEN TWO OR MORE library systems are amalgamated and a comprehensive union catalogue has been decided on, the sheer magnitude of the work involved demands much careful planning before embarking on it. Some newly-merged systems have started from scratch on entirely new catalogues, beginning at the amalgamation date and leaving the old local catalogues in use alongside the new ones until they eventually run down as the result of normal withdrawals, but this could take twenty or thirty years. Even the computer is of little assistance here in integrating pre-merger stocks, which more often than not have been classified, catalogued and even filed by different methods. The cost of retrospective computer cataloguing has been estimated in the USA at 80c per title,[1] and retrospective cataloguing for the MARC record seems to be remote, the current feasibility studies suggest.[2]

If it is decided to recatalogue the newly-combined book-stock, the best classification scheme and catalogue existing in the merging systems should be adopted as the bases to admit the stocks of the other systems, and a two-part programme of *proxy-cataloguing* and *block-revision* planned.

1 PROXY-CATALOGUING
From time to time, as normal current work permits, consecutive batches of author cards are called in from the catalogues to be revised, and checked against the ' baseline ' catalogue. The entries which are found there already as identical editions

are stencilled for the holding libraries, and the newly-notified locations are added to the ' baseline ' main cards. Those titles which are not matched up are recorded in brief on location slips to be filed in the new union name index, and the original cards are sent back to the submitting libraries for refiling there, pending the later calling-in of the books themselves in the next phase, block-revision.

The newly-printed proxy-card sets are sent to the branches where they are matched up to their books, if they are on the shelves, or their bookcards in the issue-record trays. The cataloguing department should pencil the original class notations on the card-sets to help the branches locate their books for re-carding. Those sets which cannot be matched up to books or issues after the lapse of a substantial period are returned to the cataloguing department as untraceable, and all the old entries relating to them at the branch are withdrawn as stocktaking losses; the newly-added location symbols on the ' baseline ' union cards must be deleted as well.

2 BLOCK REVISION

On the completion of the proxy phase, that is, after all the old author cards from A to Z have been matched or otherwise, a systematic subject approach can be made. Branches are asked to send in to the cataloguing department all their remaining books in progressive subject sections in the possibly different classifications; for example Dewey 000-019 and its equivalents Z in LC, M760 in Brown, and so on.

When they arrive, they are shelved together in one author sequence, keeping editions together, and are checked by the stock editor for condition, redundancy and suitability for re-location to the less-well-endowed branches with their new sets of cards, and the next subject-section called in. The temporary location slips previously filed in the union name index during the proxy phase will, of course, be automatically thrown out by the new name cards; these location slips must not be over-looked when local entries are withdrawn at the branches, in the interim before their subject-sections are called in for re-cataloguing.

One of the many problems arising from the amalgamation of library catalogues is that we must expect to encounter differing filing methods around the branches of the new system. Some of the staffs may have been trained in the ' word-by-word ' routine, and others the ' letter-by-letter '; this will result in hopeless confusion when the staff are moved around among other libraries in the new system. A survey of existing filing methods should be among the early pre-cursors of amalgamation, or afterwards should be undertaken as soon as possible, and those best in practice and most in use (possibly) should be confirmed as standard throughout the system, and the non-conforming branches instructed to refile their existing entries accordingly. All staff should be warned, however, to check catalogues with both methods in mind for a long time to come, and to correct on sight any misplacements, in order to avoid building up duplicate sequences in the catalogues.

A manual of the new cataloguing methods and organisation must be prepared and distributed to all branches as soon as the local cataloguing rules are formulated, to acquaint all staff, both juniors and seniors, with the new standard procedure for the enlarged system. This manual should be updated by periodic amendments-sheets to keep the branches advised of any procedural alterations that are made as the new system settles down and snags appear, or improvements suggest themselves.

REFERENCES
1 Dolby, J L *and others*: *Computerized library catalogs,* MIT Press, c1969; p 39.
2 Rather, J C (*ed*): *Conversion of retrospective catalog records to machine-readable form.* Washington, 1969.

13

THE PREPARATION OF BOOKLISTS

ONE OF THE DUTIES devolving on the cataloguer is the preparation of ' additions ' lists for the general readership, and special subject-lists for particular groups of readers or for topical events—anniversaries, exhibitions, news items and so on.

PERIODICAL ADDITIONS LISTS

To be of any real value, these must reach the attention of readers within a few weeks after the publication of the listed books; in other words, they should be as regular in appearance and as up-to-date as possible. Some libraries produce their new books lists as infrequently as twice a year, and many others quarterly; lists at these intervals are a sheer waste of time and money. Their book-announcements have dawdled well behind the appearance of the books on the shelves; topical books which have a short interest-period and physical life may well have been withdrawn, or be out of circulation for binding, by the time a half-yearly list is published. The main cause of tardy list-publication is commercial printing delay. On a survey I did on London borough booklists, I found it was difficult to get a worthwhile list printed by a commercial press in less than three to four weeks, and even this was for only a meagre folder. Add to this period another fortnight spent beforehand in preparing and editing the copy, and it will be seen why many librarians prefer to make their new books announcements by typed lists on their library notice-boards.

A reasonably quick and cheap method of producing a new books handout of up to 3,000 copies is by rotary duplicator as follows:

1 The cataloguer's manuscript slips, filed away after the stencilling of the catalogue cards, are brought out each month and grouped together under interest-catching headings: ' Screen and stage ', ' Home and abroad ', ' Food and drink ', and so on. An attempt could be made to bracket together kindred topics which are sometimes separated in the classification; for example, the heading ' The wild and the tame ' would include books on both domestic and wild animals, thus drawing the attention of naturalist and pet lover alike to the complements of their interests.

2 The essential parts of each entry are underlined on the manuscript cards with coloured ink to indicate to the typist which are needed.

3 The subject groups are typed on foolscap which is checked by the cataloguer for typographic errors.

4 The foolscap sheets are cut into separate group slips, each of which is marked with its line-of-print count to indicate how much page-space it will occupy.

5 The slips are clipped to foolscap sheets folded once and put inside each other as a gathering of the required number of pages. Each opening should be given balanced line-of-print counts, verso and recto; the slips can then be pasted down to form a copy make-up and running numbers given to the pages.

6 The folds are separated into opened-out sheets again and foolscap stencils are cut accordingly; that is, two pages transversely as a folio opening. These are duplicated on an ordinary rotary duplicator, care being taken that the two sides of a sheet correspond with those in the make-up so that the finished sheets can fold one within the other in the correct page order. A Gestafax or Gestaprint cover design can be used to make the list attractive, and each month's issue might have a different-coloured cover to indicate currency. The life of a monthly list

is too short to warrant the time and money spent on stapling the sheets together.

A print-order of 3,000 copies (the maximum use from a stencil) of a twenty four page monthly booklist has been produced by this method in as short a period as a week, from manuscript card to folded booklist on the library counters. This was at a time when cataloguing work was light; when the work-load is heavy, other clerical staff should be brought in to take over when the cataloguer has made his selection from his MS cards. The cost in this case, too, was less than half that of a jobbing printer's estimate, and production was six times as fast.

SPECIAL SUBJECT-LISTS

As custodian of the union catalogue, the cataloguer is often asked to prepare topical booklists; for example ' Space travel ' at the time of the moon landings, and ' Dickens ', at the centenary of his death. These subject-lists are naturally confined to books in stock at the library, and the work of compiling them can be of further use in revealing subject-gaps in the stock— a point which the compiler does well to keep constantly in mind. The lists are taken from the classified catalogue, but it is useful to examine the actual books also, for their physical condition, before advertising them to readers, and to frame suitable annotations on each which a special subject-list deserves. These class-lists can be duplicated in attractive Gestafax or Gestaprint covers, in the same fashion as the monthly additions lists are produced.

INDEX